SONG OF SONGS

Dianne Bergant

SONG OF SONGS

The Love Poetry of Scripture

Spiritual Commentaries

New City Press
Hyde Park, NY

Published in the United States by New City Press
202 Cardinal Rd., Hyde Park, NY 12538
©1998 Città Nuova, Rome, Italy, published first in Italian translation as
Il Libro del Cantico dei Cantici

Cover design by Nick Cianfarani
Cover art: "Peace on Earth." Limited editions of cover illustration available from
Lee Shapiro, 836 Vine St., Aspen, CO 81611. Used with permission.

Library of Congress Cataloging-in-Publication Data:
Bergant, Dianne.
    Song of Songs : the love poetry of Scripture / Dianne Bergant.
       p. cm.
    Includes bibliographical references.
    ISBN 1-56548-100-3
    1. Bible.   O.T.   Song of Solomon—Commentaries   I. Title.
  BS1485.3.B46   1998
  223'.9077—dc21   98-36092

2d printing: September 2001

Printed in Canada

Contents

Introduction

Interpretation of the Book

Among all of the books of the Old Testament, the Song of Songs is one of the most intriguing. On the one hand, its unabashed sensuality has captured the imagination of and has endeared it to those who appreciate passionate human love. On the other hand, more demure readers have frequently been chagrined by its erotic character and have chosen a metaphorical reading. The history of the book's interpretation demonstrates the long-standing endorsement of both reactions. Down through the ages, both Jewish and Christian interpreters have delighted in the profligate imagery of the book's songs, but they have also frequently reverted to allegory in their interpretations.

The early rabbinic writings reveal a controversy surrounding the canonicity of the book. Actually, it was not the fact of the inclusion of the Song of Songs that was at issue, as was the case with Qoheleth, but the grounds for its inclusion. For very different reasons, both books seem to have posed problems: "Did Qoheleth 'defile the hands' [was it too sacred to touch]? *Why* did the Song of Songs 'defile the hands'?" Rabbi Akiba championed the Song's canonicity by arguing:

> Heaven forbid! No one in Israel ever disputed that the Song of Songs defiles the hands. All the world is not worth the day that the Song of Songs was given to Israel; all the writings (*Ketûbîm*) are holy but the Song of Songs is the holy of holies. If they [the rabbis] differed at all, it was about Qoheleth. (Mishna Yadaim, 3:5)

It was at this same time that Akiba also condemned the practice of using the Song as a drinking ditty:

> Whoever trills his voice singing the Song of Songs in a banquet hall, regarding it a common song of praise, has no part in the world to come. (Tosefta Sanhedrin, 12:10; cf. Babylonia Talmud Sanhedrin, 101a)

This condemnation suggests that the Song was originally understood literally, as a collection of love poems.

Though initially disputed, there was eventual agreement about the sacred character of the Song of Songs; it was its meaning that remained enigmatic. Several interpretations have been advanced, each one clearly dependent upon the literary classification to which the book is assigned. Most of these interpretations can be classified in any one of four basic ways: as a dramatic performance; as an allegory; as a cultic reenactment; and as a collection of love poems.

Each of these approaches reveals distinctive facets of the Song of Songs and opens up corresponding possibilities for understanding its message. However, inconsistencies within the book itself challenge the claim of single authorship and throw into question the accuracy of interpreting it according to any strict, literary pattern, be that well-structured drama, allegory or cultic reenactment. Even among those who regard the Song of Songs as a collection of love poems, there are divergent views about its literary design and the number of poems that comprise it. While many commentators believe that the book is merely a collection of unrelated poems, others, using various literary approaches, detect a certain literary unity within it. In the final analysis, the designation of genre may come as much, or perhaps even more, from the reader than from the text itself.

The history of interpretation shows that the allegorical and/or mystical interpretive approaches lent themselves to a spiritual understanding of the Song of Songs. Although the earliest Jewish readings seem to have been literal, which led some to use it as a drinking song, both the Jewish and the Christian groups soon espoused an allegorical approach that reflected aspects of the covenantal relationship between the YHWH and Israel or God and the Church. The Jewish approach was a kind of historical allegory, recounting Israel's story from the experience of the Exodus to the advent of the messiah. The Christian allegory was either ecclesiological, describing the relationship between Christ and the Church, tropological, with moral implications, or Mariological, seeing the Virgin Mary as the preeminent type of the Church. A recent study interprets the book as a program for bringing back Davidic rule after the exile.

As early as Origen (c. 240 C.E.), Christians began to read the book with devotional eyes that saw the relationship described there as one of spiritual marriage between God and the individual soul. This view was endorsed by such influential authors as Gregory of Nyssa, Jerome, Ambrose, Theodoret, and Cyril of Alexandria. It took on added significance in the mysticism of the Middle Ages with the writings of Gregory the Great, William of Saint Thierry, Venerable Bede, Bernard of Clairvaux, as well as the sixteenth century writers Teresa of Avila and John of the Cross. A comparable allegorical approach is also found in Jewish writers such as Philo of Alexandria and Maimonides.

Spiritual interpretations of the Song of Songs usually include some form of allegory or typology. When allegory is employed, the nature imagery and exchange between the lovers are read as double entendre, saying one thing but meaning another. In a typological approach, the book is read literally as an account of human love, but this love is seen as a type of the love that God has for humankind. With the advent of critical scholarship, allegorical or typological interpretations have generally given way to literal readings, though they are still widespread among Protestant evangelicals and found within some traditions of spiritual theology.

Critical scholarship has brought us back to a literal reading of the Song of Songs. The book is now regarded as a collection of love poetry, and it is normally interpreted as such. Its sensuous imagery and its depiction of an erotic affair celebrate the passion of heterosexual love. Its explicit sexuality, along with the fact that there is no mention of God in the poems nor is there any moral teaching evident, may have contributed to its early allegorical interpretation, but such an interpretive approach is seldom promoted by scholars.

Contemporary Spirituality

A literal reading of the straightforward eroticism of the Song of Songs may pose a challenge for some who turn to the book as a biblical resource for spirituality. In such a situation, much depends upon how spirituality is understood. Today spirituality is variously defined as "the way in which a person understands and lives within his or her historical context that aspect of his or her religion, philosophy or ethic that is viewed as the loftiest, the noblest, the most calculated to lead to the fullness of the ideal or perfection being sought" (Principe, 1983:136); or as "the experience of consciously striving to integrate one's life in terms not of isolation and self-absorption but of self-transcendence toward the ultimate value one perceives" (Schneiders, 1986:266; 1988:684). It is clear from such definitions that spirituality today presumes integration of all aspects of human existence and is conversant with one's fundamental worldview.

An intrinsic element of a healthy contemporary worldview is one's understanding of sexuality. In this regard, the present generation has seen a marked concern for reuniting sexuality with the experience of the sacred. Not satisfied with a disembodied understanding of the faith, it is interested in the ways the experiences of one's sexuality influences one's

10

religious perspective. There is a definite move away from a theology that sets up a false dichotomy between spirit and matter—and that is considered by many to be one of the roots of sexism, racism, and tyranny toward the ecosystem— to an appreciation of incarnational integrity. Since the heart of biblical spirituality is love of God and love of the other, and since sexuality is the physiological and psychological grounding of the human ability to love, sexuality plays a very important role in spirituality. Therefore, in order to be meaningful in the contemporary world, any spiritual inter- pretation of the Song of Songs will necessarily have to flow from a worldview that sees sexuality as an integral compo- nent of spirituality.

A second characteristic of a contemporary spirituality, one that is even more fundamental than the first, is a deep and abiding respect for nature. We may be a unique dimension of the natural world, but we are not separate from it. We are part of it, and it is part of us. We are embedded in nature, in the creative matrix that has given and continues to give us life, and nature is also embedded in us. "We are truly children of the universe, made of the same stuff as the mountains and the rain, the sand and the stars. We are governed by the laws of life and growth and death as are the birds and the fish and the grass of the field. We thrive in the warmth of and through the agency of the sun as does every other living thing. We come from the earth as from a mother, and we are nourished from this same source of life" (Bergant, 1992:28).

Theory of Interpretation

In recent years, interpreters have acknowledged the diffi- culty in translating the theology of the biblical tradition for contemporary believers. Concerns and challenges differ from culture to culture, from generation to generation, from world

11

to world. How to be faithful to the meaning of the biblical message and yet true to the reality of the contemporary world continues to be a challenge. This challenge is certainly felt in the realm of spirituality.

Biblical critics are indebted to theorists like Hans-Georg Gadamer and Paul Ricoeur, who have provided ways of understanding the dynamics of interpretation. Gadamer believed that there is a fundamental connection between a work of art (a text) and the one experiencing it (the reader). He insisted that something is truly a work of art, not in itself in isolated majesty (an object), but only when it transforms the one who experiences it (an event). In itself, its artistic essence resides only as potential truth, ready to be recognized by the one experiencing it.

When the one perceiving the artistic work belongs to a particular historical moment with its own tradition and understanding which are different from that of the historical moment of the artist, tension develops between familiarity and strangeness, between continuity and discontinuity. Gadamer resolved this tension by introducing the notion of dialogue or conversation between the text and the reader. According to him, biblical interpretation is really a kind of dynamic dialogue between the text and the reader.

In his analysis, Gadamer distinguished among three different worlds: the world *behind* the text (the actual world of the author), the world *of* the text (the world created by the author), and the world *in front* of the text (the new world of meaning made possible by interpretation). According to him, understanding takes place when the horizon of the world projected by the text meets and interacts with the horizon of the reader. What results is a "fusion of horizons." The reader is absorbed by the story and changed by it. From the perspective of spirituality, this would be the fusion of the spiritual horizon projected by the religious message and the spiritual horizon of the reader.

Building on Gadamer's theory of interpretation, Ricoeur

12

points out differences between oral conversation and the interpretation of texts. In oral speech there is an immediacy between the speaker and the hearer. This immediacy enables the speaker to make certain that the hearer not only grasps the *sense* of the communication but is aware of the *reference* intended. The speaker is there to correct any misunderstanding.

On the other hand, a written text is removed from this immediacy in three ways: 1) Once it is written, it exists by itself, without the author to throw light on its meaning. 2) It is also removed from the original audience and is available to a limitless number of readers. 3) It can be carried beyond cultural and generational boundaries and convey its message in very diverse contexts. This distancing makes interpretation necessary, for, while the text may still make sense, it has no specific reference and is open to a variety of referents. The variety of possible readers produces what Ricoeur calls the "surplus of meaning" (Ricoeur, 1976). Since readers read from different horizons, a text can yield an array of different meanings without compromising its literary integrity.

Gadamer has been criticized for his uncritical acceptance of everything about the biblical tradition. He did not consider the gender, racial, social or political biases that it contains and projects. Ricoeur, on the other hand, agreed with Freud that the force and meaning of language can conceal a false consciousness. Refining Freud's "hermeneutics of suspicion," Ricoeur went on to develop a way of reading that is open to the possibilities of the future while aware of the limitations of the past.

It seems obvious that the world is known only through the particular perspective of the knower. In reading, the world of the text is perceived and understood through the lens of the social location of the reader. Until recently readers have not always been self-conscious about their social location. Those who enjoy positions of power, whether political, economic or even academic, have often accepted their perspective as normative for all. Groups within society that enjoy limited or no power at all are still socialized into this dominant worldview. However, their social location, considered marginal within the dominant culture, provides them with a significantly different perception of the values and standards of the dominant worldview.

Social location plays a determinative role in interpretation. To claim that a reading is neutral is to support uncritically the perspective of the dominant status quo and to perpetuate its biases. On the other hand, in a context of inequality, a particular reading can be more inclusive or liberative in at least one of two ways. Either the major theological questions arise and are answered from within the actual experience of marginality or oppression or a stand in solidarity with the marginal or oppressed is taken and theology is developed out of that stand.

All of the factors explained above have influenced the method of interpretation employed within this commentary of the Song of Songs. It will follow the literal reading of the text as promoted by the majority of critical scholars today. It will employ a "hermeneutic of suspicion" particularly sensitive to issues of race or ethnic origin, class and gender, acknowledging at the outset that another focus might yield another understanding, thus contributing to a "surplus of meaning." In keeping with the intent of this commentary series, it will read the text with an eye to the possibilities it offers for contemporary spirituality, enabling a "fusion of horizons."

The Structure of the Book

While the literary composition of the Song of Songs is not the principal concern of this study, a decision regarding its structure is the first step in any serious analysis. It is debatable whether literary unity should be claimed on the basis of identical themes and imagery, since love poems generally share such characteristics. Nonetheless, similarity of style, the repetition of patterns, a coherent plot and consistency in characters' behavior all suggest some kind of literary unity in the final form of the book. Commentators who argue for literary coherence frequently group individual poems into distinct units based on characterization, plot, or literary pattern. The same criteria are used by those who view the book as a collection of discrete poems. This procedure has led to great disparity in enumeration, ranging from five to fifty-two poems. The following literary structure has been adopted here: 1:1; 1:2–2:7; 2:8–3:5; 3:6–5:1; 5:2–6:3; 6:4–8:4; 8:5-14. This structure is based on identification of both speakers and literary patterns. An explanation for this decision follows.

The superscription (1:1) is clearly set off from the rest of the book. The first and second units (1:2–2:7; 2:8–3:5) are delineated by the same final solemn adjuration directed toward the daughters of Jerusalem (2:7; 3:5). The third unit (3:6–5:1), which begins with a poem that is clearly independent of what precedes it, is praise of his loved one by the man, while the fourth (5:2–6:3) is comparable praise by the woman. The fifth unit (6:4–8:4) is delineated by the solemn adjuration found earlier (8:4; cf. 2:7; 3:5). What remains (8:5-14) seems to be a collection of disparate poems. The book will be examined with this structure in view.

Form critical study has provided genre classification which can assist in understanding this rather complex literary creation. The material can be identified as: poems of yearning (1:2-4; 2:6; 7:9b-10; 8:1-3); self-descriptions (1:5-6; 8:10), poems of admiration (1:9-17; 2:3; 4:9-15; 6:4-5a; 7:8-11); accounts of an experience (2:8-10a; 3:1-5; 5:2-8; 6:11-12; 8:5b); characterizations of the physical charms of the loved one, similar to the Arabic *wasf* (4:1-7; 5:10-16; 6:5b-7; 7:2-8); invitations to tryst (2:10b-14; 4:8; 5:1; 7:12-14.

I

The Song of Songs, Which is of Solomon

Opening Verse (1:1)

¹:¹ The Song of Songs by Solomon.

The opening verse of the book is a superscription that performs several significant functions: It identifies the book as a song; it graces it with honorific prestige; and it affixes Solomonic authority to its message. This is a lyric song, not a religious song. While at least thirty other biblical psalms are identified in this way, with the exception of Psalm 46 all are also labeled religious song or psalm. The singular form used here suggests that the editor who appended this superscription intended that, regardless of its original form and meaning, the collection in its final form should be regarded as a literary unit.

The Hebrew form of "Song of Songs" is a superlative construct intended to set this song apart from all other songs. Of all the lyric poems of the Bible, this particular one is the most sublime song, the song above all songs. The designation is quite interesting when one remembers that the Song is about passionate human love and not religious or political matters, as is the case with the biblical psalms. In other words, the one lyric song that is above all other songs is erotic in nature.

Literally translated, the superscription reads: "The Song

16

of Songs, which is Solomon's." The Hebrew form lends itself to two different understandings. Either this is a song that comes from the mouth of Solomon or in some way it belongs to the Judean king. Although he is explicitly mentioned six times in various places (1:5; 3:7,9,11; 8:11,12), Solomon himself plays no significant role in the Song. Instead, he has become a symbol of wealth, a standard of comparison. The commentary that follows will show that the poems describe mostly the woman's perspective in the love relationship and not the man's. All of this suggests that this reference to Solomon should be understood in the latter sense, that is, as an association with Solomon other than actual authorship.

Most likely, the superscription confers Solomonic authority on the message of the book in the same way as superscriptions confer such authority on many of the Proverbs (e.g., Prv 1:1; 10:1; 25:1). One must ask: Why would a collection of love lyrics be accorded Solomonic legitimation? Was this the only way for it to garner official approval? Some commentators propose that the tradition about Solomon's wives and concubines (1 Kgs 11:3) invited such a link. As interesting as it may be, this explanation only addresses a possible historical link; it does not explain why the book was ultimately included in the list of sacred writings in the first place. We face today the same question that faced the rabbis at the time of Akiba: Why did the Song of Songs "defile the hands"? However one explains these issues, the collection of love poems enjoys not only canonical status but also Solomonic legitimation; their message is considered authoritative wisdom.

Solomonic legitimation places the Song of Songs in the category of wisdom literature. The primary interest of that tradition is instruction in the proper ways of living. The sages were humanists, concerned with human beings and attentive to human welfare, values and dignity. They taught that whatever benefited humankind was a good to be pursued, and whatever was harmful should be avoided and con-

17

demned. Training of any kind, whether within the family or the court, or in preparation for a profession, sought to impart the skills needed to succeed in the respective arena. The criterion for judging the value of any undertaking was the degree of well-being that it provided.

The wisdom teachers did not advocate the pursuit of happiness for its own sake. Happiness or success was believed to be a by-product of an upright life. Since the sages regarded well-being and happiness as evidence that one's life and behavior were in accord with the order of creation, success was considered concrete evidence of the wisdom or right-eousness of the person who succeeded. There were usually very definite lessons that the sages wanted to teach, lessons about cosmic, familial or civic order. Their teachings frequently contained an oblique "the moral of the story is . . ."

Although the wise women and men believed that there was a proper way of behaving, they did not insist on a rigid standard that would fit every circumstance. They acknowledged that varying circumstances made each case unique. In fact, only those who were able to evaluate the situation and decide on the best course of action were considered wise. The truly sagacious person was the one who could draw on a store of wisdom gained from life experience, and who knew which course of action fitted which situation. Placing the Song of Songs within the wisdom tradition suggests that it contains lessons beneficial for right living, insights that will enhance human life. A careful examination of these erotic poems will uncover what these lessons might be.

II

Mutual Longing

The first unit of the Song (1:2–2:7) consists of a lyric poem spoken by the woman (1:2-6) and a series of poems wherein the couple individually proclaim their admiration for each other (1:7–2:7). The shift between second- and third-person pronouns utilized here (1:7–2:7)—a poetic device called *enallage*—has been the source of much confusion. This device is found frequently in the poetry of the ancient world. Understanding this literary feature resolves the confusion caused by the change of voice at several points in the poem (e.g., 1:8).

Yearnings of Love (1:2-6)

B^1 [2] Let him kiss me with kisses of his mouth!

More delightful is your love than wine!
   [3] Your name spoken is a spreading perfume—
that is why the maidens love you.
[4] Draw me!—

D   We will follow you eagerly!

B   Bring me, O king, to your chambers.

---

1.   The marginal letters indicate the speaker of the verses: *B*—Bride; *D*—Daughters of Jerusalem; *G*—Bridegroom.

D   With you we rejoice and exult,
        we extol your love; it is beyond wine:
        how rightly you are loved!

B   ⁵I am as dark—but lovely,
        O daughters of Jerusalem—
    As the tents of Kedar,
        as the curtains of Salma.
    ⁶Do not stare at me because I am swarthy,
        because the sun has burned me.
    My brothers have been angry with me;
        they charged me with the care of the vineyards:
        my own vineyard I have not cared for.

The initial lyric of the woman bespeaks intense longing. The imagery that describes her desire is vividly sensuous, appealing to both taste and smell, the sensations of which frequently coalesce. First the woman cries out for her beloved's kisses. Since the mouth could be regarded as a primary physical gateway to the interior of the person, passionate mouth kissing literally opens the lovers to each other. Such openness renders one dangerously vulnerable, capable of being entered into and possessed by the other, as well as entering into and losing oneself within the other. Only audacious trust can dispose one to such vulnerability. From the outset, the Song of Songs paints a picture of human passion at its best, trusting and open to another in unguarded love.

This poem is not simply an exaltation of physical yearning for the pleasure that comes with passionate kissing. Rather, it is a song of longing that springs from genuine ardent love. The Hebrew word used here for love is a form of *dôd*, a term of endearment. Some form of the word is found thirty-three times in the Song and only in reference to the man. An Akkadian equivalent, which means "beloved" or "darling" and is also reserved for men, occasionally appears in that literature as part of a royal epithet. This specific connotation might help to explain some of the other references and allusions to royalty that are found in the Song (1:4, 12, 17; 3:6-11; 7:1, 5). The use of the word by the woman is a clear expression of her devotion and the exalted regard in which she holds her beloved. (In many translations, the man is referred to as the active lover and the woman as the passive beloved. This seems to be a bias of the translators rather than the meaning of the Hebrew words themselves. Since the woman in the Song is quite active in her love, the word *dôd* will always be rendered "beloved" in this commentary.)

Too often commentators have overlooked the theological value of human love as described in the Song of Songs. They consider it to be a mere shadow of divine love and claim that its true value lies in its ability to move beyond itself to some kind of transcendence of the human realm. Such a perspective falls far short of an adequate appreciation of incarnational theology, which considers human love as both a value in itself and a sign or symbol of divine love and claims that we love God precisely in the act of loving others. In other words, God is not found beyond human endeavor but at the very heart of it. This perspective is not espousing some form of pantheism which makes no distinction between the human and the divine. It is more a case of recognizing that God is actively involved in human existence, though not confined as we are by its constraints.

Centuries ago Irenaeus wrote that "The glory of God is in the human person fully alive." One is never more alive than when in a relationship of love. The virtues that identify a holy person are the attitudes called forth from us by such a relationship. They include: courage, vulnerability, defenselessness, mutual respect, unselfishness, fidelity, to name but a few. These are the very virtues that manifest themselves in the love that unfolds before us in the poetry of the Song of Songs.

Reflecting on her love, the woman declares that it is better than wine. While wine is a staple of Israelite life, the two

21

images of luxuriance that follow this comparison (v. 3) suggest that its intoxicating nature is the intended focus here. Her beloved's love transports her; his name, the essence of his personality, is aromatic, rich in itself and transfusing its surroundings with its bouquet. The imagery is extravagant. She tastes his kisses; she is intoxicated by his love; she is imbued with the fragrance of his being. She is so taken by love that she can taste it and smell it. Furthermore, she is not the only one enamored by this man. According to her, other young women are enthralled by him as well.

A second time the woman voices her desire, longing to be with her beloved who is here characterized as a king (see reference to *dôd*, v. 2). What appears to be a description of union (being together in his chamber), is probably an expression of her anticipation and imagination. Once again the love of this man is deemed more intoxicating than wine (cf. v. 2). The woman is obsessed with him and, like lovers everywhere, she believes that other marriageable women recognize and applaud the charms that have so captivated her (v. 4; cf. v. 3).

The woman now turns to the daughters of Jerusalem, residents of the city (vv. 5f). The identity of these daughters is not clear. They are directly involved only with the woman and not with the man. They act as a kind of foil for her. Since there are no real soliloquies in the Song, she is most likely addressing them when it is clear that she is not speaking to the man. They pose questions (3:6; 5:9; 6:1) to which she provides answers, thus facilitating the forward movement of the dialogue. She appeals to them not to judge her by the darkness of her complexion (1:6), not to interrupt the couple's lovemaking (2:7; 3:5), and not to tell the man that she is sick with love for him (5:8).

Speaking to these daughters of Jerusalem, the woman unabashedly attests to her own comeliness (vv. 5f). A good bit of debate surrounds the nature of the darkness of her complexion. At issue is whether black refers to skin tone or to race. Most commentators opt for the former. This interpretation is supported by the text itself, which explains her dark color as the result of exposure to the sun (1:6). Still there does seem to be some sort of discrimination here, perhaps a class bias, for the woman defends her coloring. Unlike the sheltered women of the elite (the daughters of Jerusalem?), lower class women were required to work outdoors, subjecting themselves to the elements. Despite what these daughters might have thought, the favorable depiction of the woman indicates that the author explicitly disavows any class bias.

The woman compares her dark coloring to the goat-haired nomadic tents of Kedar, the tribe that sprang from Ishmael (Gn 36:11) and that eventually came to be known for its opulence (Is 49:28; Ez 27:21). This particular tribe may have been mentioned because of this suggestion of wealth, or because its name constitutes a simple word play on another Hebrew word for black (*qdar*). The woman's color also resembles the curtains that hung in the wilderness tabernacle (cf. Ex 26:1-13; 36:8-17), ascribed anachronistically to Solomon. These two similes are employed as evidence that dark coloring does not always denote inferiority. In fact, it is sometimes associated with great wealth.

The woman herself may be unapologetic regarding her coloring, but it appears to have been the object of the scrutiny of the daughters of Jerusalem. She asks that they not stare at her, and she explains that her swarthiness is the result of exposure to the intense rays of the sun to which she was subject (v. 6). The Song only now makes mention of the woman's family. Nowhere in the book is there a reference to her father. Her brothers seem to have assumed responsibility for her (1:6; 8:8), a practice quite common in patriarchal societies. The phrase "sons of my mother" (a better translation of the Hebrew) suggests full rather than half brothers, children of the same mother with whom she should be able to enjoy a special closeness. This closeness is most likely one of kinship rather than emotional attachment. It may be this very bond of kinship that explains their protective attitude toward her, a protectiveness which she spurns.

The theme of the vineyard is rich in meaning. On the literal level, it represents one of the most common and most profitable occupations of the Near East. The grapes and raisins that a vineyard yields and the wine produced from its fruit are staples of the diet. For this reason, the vine became a symbol of basic sustenance (cf. 1 Kgs 4:25; 2 Kgs 18:31; Mi 4:4) and even of prosperity (Dt 8:8). On another level, the fruitfulness of the vine became a simile of the sexual fecundity of the woman (cf. Ps 128:3; Ez 19:10). Perhaps the most familiar personified characterization of vineyard is found in the famous poem in Isaiah (5:1-7). There the loved one (Israel) is metaphorically depicted as a vineyard.

This many-faceted understanding of vineyard is found in the Song as well. Here the woman speaks of two different vineyards. The ownership of the first is not mentioned, but the second is identified as belonging to her (v. 6). While it is true that women did on occasion claim ownership of land, it was only when there were no legitimate male heirs, and this exception was considered necessary in order to assure that the land not be lost to the family inheritance (cf. Jos 17:3f). Such would not be the case here, for it was precisely her male siblings who put her in charge of the vineyards. While the first vineyard probably should be understood literally, here and elsewhere in the Song (8:12) the woman's vineyard appears to be a symbol of her sexuality.

In this self-affirmation, the play on the word vineyard moves the poem from an explanation of the woman's coloring, which may have been the occasion of the disdain of the daughters of Jerusalem, to a reference to what is perceived as sexual irresponsibility, the reason for her brothers' outrage. It is not clear whether or not the couple ever really consummate their love. While there is not explicit mention of coitus, many of the double entendres suggest that such an

24

understanding is intended. The reference to the woman's vineyard is one such instance. However the allusion is understood, it is important to note that while characters within the poems may react negatively to the woman's behavior, nothing in the Song suggests that the poet considers it unbecoming.

The Song of the Soul : In a way, spirituality might be considered the song of the soul. It is the unique manifestation of the soul's lofty and noble ideals, the creative expression of the human person fully alive. Different times and different cultures espouse various ideals and address various issues. All of this goes into shaping a spirituality and providing a spiritual lens through which to view the world and everything within it.

This first lyric poem of praise and longing demonstrates several characteristics found in a contemporary spirituality. The first and most evident characteristic is the way it portrays the woman according to standards of self-approval, self-definition, and self-determination. The second characteristic flows from the first; it is the mutual nature of the relationship of love depicted in the poems. The woman is an active partner in this love, not merely the object of the man's desire and attention. The third characteristic is a sensitivity to the intrinsic value of the entire natural world. Although the integrity of creation is fundamental to everything, it is not always uppermost in human consciousness. Contemporary spirituality seeks to correct this oversight.

Reading the poem from this threefold perspective, a very interesting picture emerges. First, contrary to the image of the withdrawn and passive damsel who, like a shrinking violet, retreats into some protective place of safety, this woman is bold and forthright in the pursuit of her love. Hers is both an incarnational and a nature-sensitive spirituality. She is not intimidated by the earthiness of life and love, nor by the very natural desires that she experiences. It is clear that she relishes human emotion. It is also clear that she appreciates the way the natural world dazzles the senses, for she moves easily from her own experience of sensual emotion to an expression of sensuous delight. Still she is not a captive of her emotion. Rather, its intensity is a gauge of the depth of her admiration of the marvelous qualities of the one she loves.

There is a very important dimension to the erotic kissing for which the woman longs. Without in any way minimizing the pleasure that both she and the man she loves will enjoy, the vulnerability that accompanies this pleasure should be noted. Passionate lovemaking creates a kind of ecstasy that removes all inhibitions and leaves one unguarded. Such vulnerability can be risked only where there is some form of trust. The intensity of the pleasure is measured by the degree of trust and self-giving that one is willing to invest in the other. The self-giving of one lover results in the pleasure of the other and engenders reciprocal self-giving.

In addition to this, the woman has a very healthy acceptance of her physical appearance. She rejects a notion of beauty that seems to be based on a discriminatory perception (vv. 5f). Although there is a color bias here, it appears to be more along the lines of class than of race or ethnic origin. Though not evident here, there are other biases that cause women to question their God-given natural beauty, biases that must be identified and eradicated. They may differ according to culture, but they are often based on racial characteristics such as bone structure, skin coloring or hair texture. These biases may also reflect a preference for youth with its firmness or lissomeness of body, and the absence of wrinkles. Body shape and size are also constitutive to various stereotypes of physical beauty.

Such stereotypes develop out of the choice of one or two combinations of physical features at the cost of rejecting all others. While there is nothing wrong with preferring certain characteristics, to deem others unacceptable and to treat

26

people in a discriminatory manner because of them is to disdain the ingenuity of the Creator who has fashioned each person in a unique way. While it is true that the real value of a person does not reside in his or her bodily appearance, we should never minimize the importance of one's physical constitution, for it is integral to one's self-concept and, ultimately, to one's very being.

Contemporary spirituality neither glorifies nor scorns the body with its many-faceted reality. Rather, it embraces it as coming from God; it stands in awe of the countless ways that human beauty is manifested; and it demonstrates its gratitude for this diversity by accepting first one's own physical appearance and then the physical appearances of all others. Since stereotypical female beauty is a preoccupation of many cultures, this accepting attitude toward the body has become a central characteristic of contemporary thought. Male stereotypes may emphasize different features, but they are nonetheless discriminatory and self-defacing for men, and they too tend to limit our appreciation of the way human beings are embedded in the natural world. Respect for the body, though often linked to gender issues, is really more broadly a matter of sensitivity to nature, a second characteristic of contemporary spirituality.

Another feature of this poem is the woman's unwillingness to conform to patriarchal strictures that lie behind the reaction of her brothers. She seems undeterred by their disapproval of her behavior, a disapproval that seems to have less to do with morality than with social convention. Motivated by genuine love, she moves beyond the custom that may guarantee security but also imposes confinement to a more independent plain, which offers self-reliance but which also requires personal responsibility. Her autonomy is not the emancipation of disobedience but that of maturity. Such self-possession and commitment to reality as honestly perceived, despite the risks involved, is highly valued by contemporary spirituality.

Finally, it must be noted that none of the features singled out here is in any way denounced by the poet. On the contrary, the teaching of the poems is considered to be appropriate wisdom instruction, having been accorded Solomonic legitimation. Furthermore, the very title of the collection suggests that this is the most sublime song, the song beyond all others. Its teaching can certainly be called the song of the soul.

Reflections on this first part of the Song of Songs highlight two aspects of human reality: deep human emotion, particularly love; and physical appearance.

Like the woman in the Song, our own human emotion springs from some hidden source deep within us. It is a gauge of our response to the world of which we are a part. It comes from God, and it opens a window into the way we react to whatever touches our lives. It tells us what we love and what we fear, what we want and what we disdain. Emotion adds color and texture to our lives. It heightens our senses and gives perspective to our thoughts.

There is no emotion that can transform us like human love is able to do. It can take a monochromatic world and change it into technicolor brilliance. It can make everything we touch exciting and comforting. It can bring adventure to the most mundane. It can attune us to the secret music of the universe. It is through human love that God opens for us the sensuous treasures of the world.

Like the woman in the Song, we too must unabashedly accept our own physical appearance. We do not choose our basic physical features; we inherit them. In a sense, we are but a strand in the complex yet delicate web of life. In our bodies we carry the history of our families, of our race. Our bone structure, the shape of our eyes, the color of our skin, the texture of our hair all demonstrate the ingenious flexibility placed by the creator into the very core of the human cell. Our ancestors before us adapted to the circumstances of their environment, and we carry the print of that adaptation in our bodies. Each one of us is a unique work of art, brought forth from the womb of the world. When we behold ourselves, we can only stand in awe before the creative imagination of nature.

Love's Dialogue (1:7–2:7)

B   ⁷Tell me, you whom my heart loves,
      where you pasture your flock,
      where you give them rest at midday,
  Lest I be found wandering
      after the flocks of your companions.

G   ⁸If you do not know,
      O most beautiful among women,
  Follow the tracks of the flock
      and pasture the young ones
      near the shepherds' camps.

G   ⁹To the steeds of Pharaoh's chariots
      would I liken you, my beloved:
  ¹⁰Your cheeks lovely in pendants,
      your neck in jewels.
  ¹¹We will make pendants of gold for you,
      and silver ornaments.

B   ¹²For the king's banquet
      my nard gives forth its fragrance.
  ¹³My lover is for me a sachet of myrrh
      to rest in my bosom.
  ¹⁴My lover is for me a cluster of henna
      from the vineyards of Engedi.

G   ¹⁵Ah, you are beautiful, my beloved,
      ah, you are beautiful; your eyes are doves!
B   ¹⁶Ah you are beautiful, my lover—
      yes, you are lovely.
  ¹⁷Our couch, too, is verdant;
      the beams of our house are cedars,
      our rafters, cypresses.

^{2:1}I am a flower of Sharon,
    a lily of the valley.

G   ²As a lily among thorns,
    so is my beloved among women.

B   ³As an apple tree among the trees of the woods,
    so is my lover among men.
  I delight to rest in his shadow,
    and his fruit is sweet to my mouth.
  ⁴He brings me into the banquet hall
    and his emblem over me is love.
  ⁵Strengthen me with raisin cakes,
    refresh me with apples,
    for I am faint with love.
  ⁶His left hand is under my head
    and his right arm embraces me.
  ⁷I adjure you, daughters of Jerusalem,
    by the gazelles and hinds of the field,
  Do not arouse, do not stir up love
    before its own time.

The next part of the Song (1:7–2:7) takes on a slightly different character. The lovers seem to be together, at least they are speaking to each other. At times the dialogue is apparent (1:7-11,15-17), at other times the speakers seem to engage in rhapsodic monologue (1:12-14; 2:1-7). These are poems of tender exclamation and mutual admiration, the kind one would expect to hear from lovers. They also repeat the motif of the woman's longing and searching.

The woman continues speaking, but now turns her attention toward the one she loves (v. 7; cf. 3:1, 2, 3, 4). Although the translation reads "whom my heart loves," a rendition closer to the Hebrew would be "whom my soul loves." There is no intended Platonic dualism here between body and soul. Although the Hebrew *nepeš* does not carry exactly the same meaning as the Greek *psyché*, they are both frequently translated as "life." The Greek refers to the whole person, with an

30

orientation toward the spiritual dimension. The Hebrew, being a much more concrete language, refers to the whole person as well, but with an orientation toward the physical but somewhat non-material source of life, the breath. The woman loves the man with her whole being.

The woman addresses the man with an imperative: Tell me where you allow your flock to rest during the heat of the day. Presumably, this is so that she can meet him there. She seems intent on joining him, and she wants to avoid wandering from pasture to pasture. The veil she would wear, should she have to go in search of him, would hide her identity from his companions, but could also miscast her as one of the prostitutes who often frequented the fields seeking a liaison. Although her yearning is intense and she is willing to place herself to some degree at risk, the woman wants to avoid having their relationship misunderstood. Their love is deep and enduring. It is not cheap and fleeting like some illicit encounter, and she does not want it to be so judged by others.

The origin of the response to this plea is difficult to interpret. The young woman is called the "most beautiful among women" (v. 8). Because this expression is used elsewhere by the daughters of Jerusalem (cf. 5:9; 6:1), some think that they are speaking here as well. However, most commentators believe that it is the man who here proclaims her extraordinary beauty. He suggests that she should just follow her own flocks and they will lead her to him. Nevertheless, this course will most likely bring her close to shepherds' tents, just where she did not want to go. Still, if she wants a rendezvous with him, she will have to risk the hostility of others. Following the urging of one's heart can be a very lonely pursuit, especially when this seems to conflict in some way with social norms or customs. The imagery in this exchange is quite straightforward and may be the clearest identification of the involvement of both the man and the woman with shepherding.

The man continues speaking, but now his words are filled with praise of his loved one's sexual attractiveness and the enhancement of her beauty that ornamentation provides (vv. 9-11). He calls her beloved (ra'yâ, v. 9), a special term of endearment used only for women and used quite consistently by him (cf. 1:15; 2:2, 10, 13; 4:1; 5:2; 6:4). He then compares her to a mare, let loose among the stallions of the Pharaoh's chariotry, whose tantalizing presence could throw these well disciplined horses into total confusion. This comparison may seem foreign and even offensive to contemporary sensitivities, but the innovative imagery is striking, and the equine frenzy that it suggests aptly illustrates his perception of the sexual irresistibility of the woman he loves.

The point of the metaphor shifts slightly, concentrating now on the mare's adornment. The bridles of Pharaoh's horses were often extravagantly decorated with tassels, fringes and trappings of ivory or precious metal, all of which added to the horses' grandeur. Since ancient Near Eastern women frequently wore jewelry on their faces and around their necks, the similarity lends itself to the comparison. Ornaments only enhance the splendor of what is already magnificent in appearance. According to the man, the beauty of his loved one is every bit as dramatic as the awe-inspiring display of the Egyptian chariotry.

The woman speaks not directly to the man but in a kind of love-monologue, a song of admiration (vv. 12-14). Returning to the theme of luxuriant aromas (cf. v. 3), she extols first her own radiant scent and then his. Mention of the king is probably another example of the custom of using royal allusions in describing lovers (cf. v. 4; 7:1, 5). This interpretation is substantiated by the double reference in this poem to beloved (dôd). The couch on which the king reclines could be used for both eating and lovemaking, thus strengthening the link between these two activities. Finally, nard is a fragrant ointment that is often used as a love-charm. Found in the region of India, its scarcity adds to its intrinsic value. The woman is describing the intoxicating pleasure that one experiences in the presence of the beloved.

Just as she is the source of his pleasure, he is the source of hers. He is compared to myrrh and henna, two exotic perfumes highly valued in the ancient Near East. Myrrh, a spicy scent made from the resin of certain trees, served as a perfume for clothing and sometimes as a medicine. It was also used to anoint priests and ritual vessels, thus conferring on it a sacred character. The henna scent was extracted from the roselike flowers of shrubbery that apparently grew abundantly at Ein-gedi, a flourishing oasis in the wilderness near the Dead Sea. Its vibrant presence in the midst of the barren desert is another allusion to the extraordinariness of this deeply loved man.

Besides mention of the couch, the sexual nature of this encounter is seen in the reference to the placement of the myrrh (the man) between the woman's breasts. The practice of wearing a sachet there was and continues to be popular in certain cultures. In this poem, the woman regards her beloved as such a captivating source of delight, pressed against her bosom in an intimate embrace. The form of the verb translated "rest" suggests a long period of time, perhaps the entire night. This is not a description of a brief though loving show of affection, but of a long and passionate embrace. The poem describes the delights that the lovers derive from each other.

Further evidence in the mutuality of this enjoyment can be seen in the way each admires the physical charms of the other. The man acclaims the beauty of his loved one (ra'yâ), emphasizing his admiration of her by repeating his declaration (v. 15). He seems particularly captivated by her eyes. The aspect of the doves that lends itself to this comparison is unclear. Some commentators believe that it is their color, others that the gentle motion of their wings resembles the fluttering eyelashes of a shy or coquettish maiden. Still others hold that the softness and delicacy of the birds is an apt metaphor of the gentle eyes of the woman. The precise point of the reference cannot be positively determined.

33

Echoing her beloved's (*dôd*) words of praise, the woman in turn unabashedly extols his beauty (v. 16a). Androcentric or male-centered societies are normally preoccupied with the way female beauty captures the attention and the imagination of men. In such instances, little if any consideration is given to the reciprocal captivation of women by the physical characteristics of men. Virtuous women are thought to have little or no interest in the contours of a man's body or in sexual arousal. Only women of loose morals or questionable virtue are so interested. Contrary to such a sexist point of view, the woman in the Song is unapologetically enraptured by the physical charms of the man, and there is no indication that either the man himself or the poet who created him is offended by her candor.

She continues with a sketch of their trysting place (vv. 16b-17), the character of which has been variously understood. The references themselves yield two different though related pictures. One interpretation suggests a room of elaborate construction, made of cedar and pine, containing a couch on which have been strewn newly cut branches. This would fit well into the royal motif so often alluded to in the Song. However, the royal motif is probably not a reference to real social status, but a metaphor that enhances the characterization of the couple.

Another explanation of the trysting place envisions a rustic setting with a makeshift booth not unlike those set up during harvest time. A slight variation of this interpretation suggests a bed of greenery in the forest surrounded by majestic cedars and scented pines. Either of these readings corresponds to the pastoral scene depicted earlier in the chapter (vv. 7f). The rustic setting seems a more plausible explanation, given the way trees and bushes are metaphorically used in the declarations of admiration that follow (2:1-3). However, whether the place of rendezvous is a luxurious room or a luxuriant spot in the woods, the grandeur of its character corresponds to the splendor of the loving encounter that occurs within it.

The pastoral scenes already depicted and the sylvan description of the trysting place inspire further vernal imagery. The woman identifies herself as a blossoming flower, first a crocus and then a lily, both sweet-smelling blooms (2:1). The exact identity of the first-mentioned flower is unknown, though it has been called a rose. A better classification might be the crocus or narcissus, hardy flowers that appear toward the end of winter and bloom through the beginning of spring. The word appears only one other place in the Bible (Is 35:1), and there, in the company of the majesty of Lebanon, Carmel and Sharon, it symbolizes the regenerative blossoming of the people. The parallelism of the verse links this flower with the lily, the blooming period of which follows that of the first flower, and which also represents the regeneration of the people (Hos 14:6f).

There is no hint here of self-abasement. These flowers may at first glance seem common, even insignificant, but they are indigenous to the land, heralds of the coming of spring, harbingers of new life. In the Song, the motif of spring suggests the blossoming of love. This is the point of comparison with these flowers. The woman is a sign of the newness of love and the regeneration of life.

The man takes up the word lily and draws another comparison with the woman (v. 2). In his eyes, even if these flowers are considered ordinary, they still outstrip whatever it is that surrounds them. In like manner, his loved one (*ra'yâ*) far surpasses all other maidens (daughters). Had they too been portrayed as flowers, no doubt he would have maintained that she is the most exquisite of all. Since she has compared herself to common blossoms, he will liken all the others to thorns and thistles. The point of this comparison is not to demean the other maidens, but to exalt his own loved one. These are the very sentiments he expressed earlier when he called her "the most beautiful among women" (1:8).

Once again the woman patterns her song of admiration after that of the man (v. 3; cf. 1:15f). As she is a flower among thorns, without peer among the maidens, he is a fruit-bearing tree in a wild woodland, without rival among the young men (sons). The exact identity of the fruit that is generally translated apple is unknown, However, since it is derived from the root for "breathe," it is thought to be of a fragrant-smelling variety. The woodland is untamed forest where only the stalwart trees thrive. These comparisons suggest that the two lovers are not only unparalleled in their desirability, but also strong enough to survive in inhospitable surroundings. These are the kinds of sentiments uttered by lovers everywhere. The loved one, regardless of who she or he might be, has no peer, is beyond all comparison.

Developing this woodland motif, the woman recounts the pleasure that she takes in the man. As previously she encircled him with her arms, holding him close to herself (1:13), now she is embraced by his shade which provides her with protection and comfort. Secure in his love, she delights in his kisses, the fruit that is sweet to her taste. The comparison of kisses with the intoxicating sweetness of wine (cf. 1:2) fits well with the image of a wine house. There the woman is led to a trysting place where the two can enjoy their love. The reference here may be metaphorical, an allusion to some rustic grove where wine could be enjoyed, but where kisses would be even more inebriating.

The next phrase (v. 4b) is difficult to understand. The verbal root means "to look" or "to behold." This yields the translation, "his look is one of love." However, the noun form which is found here is rendered "emblem" or "banner." This military image may seem out of place unless the purpose of and the insignia on the standard are understood. The standard is a sign of possession or jurisdiction. When it is unfurled, it designates the region over which control is exercised. The insignia on the standard usually depicts the identity or the purpose of the standard's owner. This being the case, whether the phrase is read "his look is one of love," or "his emblem is love," the sense is basically the same: His intention is love.

36

This is a very important statement about the aspirations of the man. Up to this point, the Song has described the amorous longing of the woman. She is the one who craves his kisses (1:2), who yearns for his presence (1:4, 7), who relishes their lovemaking (1:12f; 2:3b). Though she is speaking here, she is describing *his* intentions, which are as amorous as are hers.

The motif of tasting, an image of lovemaking, is taken up again (v. 5). Faint with love, the woman asks for food to sustain her. The meaning of this verse is disputed. Some commentators maintain that the food is intended as nourishment. However, since food and wine have already been used metaphorically in the Song, such a reading seems more appropriate here as well. The type of refreshment that the woman requests is significant. Raisins are akin to wine, since they both come from the grape. In the Song, wine suggests passionate kissing. The apples are the fruit of the very tree to which the man is compared (v. 3). Apples, then, allude to the man himself. This reading suggests that faint with love the woman asks for the only thing that can refresh her, the delights of lovemaking itself.

The description that follows (v. 6) is of a classic position in which lovers are portrayed. Though the verb is translated "embrace," the action involves the use of the hands rather than the arms. With the left hand he holds her; with the right he embraces or fondles her. All of her yearning has been realized. He has brought her to the place of lovemaking; he takes her in his arms; he begins to make love. The easy movement from songs of yearning to expressions of admiration leave doubt as to whether this is a description of an actual encounter or an example of the woman's fantasizing. Both interpretations have been advanced.

The closing refrain (2:7) is a solemn adjuration directed to the daughters of Jerusalem. The gazelle mentioned is an animal known for its beauty, agility and sexual potency; the hind is clearly identified as untamed and free. These are two apt images for these lovers. However, several commentators believe that the phrase is really a circumlocution that avoids using the name of God in this solemn oath. The exact meaning of the request is unclear. It seems to be asking that the daughters do nothing to stimulate love before its time. However, the adjuration follows a description of the lovers in a passionate embrace and so there is no need to warn against untimely arousal. There the phrase may simply function as a refrain, separating one unit of the Song from another. Its disjunction with what precedes it serves to heighten the uneven movement from yearning to enjoyment to separation and further pursuit.

The Song of the Soul: Several components of this dialogue resonate with aspects of a contemporary spirituality. Despite the fact that they are so much a part of each other that they cannot be easily isolated, three aspects will be examined in turn in order to appreciate the implications of each. First there is the unabashed sensuality. Although the lovers and their desires are seen primarily through the eyes of the woman, both lovers are depicted as uninhibited in their expressions of passion and in their longing for union. Kissing, embracing and fondling are described in ways that underscore and even exaggerate their amorous character. Nothing in the poems suggests that such candid eroticism is unseemly. Instead, it appears very natural and quite honorable.

Like nothing else in life, erotic love in its straining for union reveals humankind's rudimentary social character. In the Song it lays bare the woman's fundamental need for the other, as well as her craving to give of herself without reserve. Although she hoped to find her own pleasure in him, love stripped her of her defenses and she surrendered herself to vulnerability, trusting that she would be gently cherished as she gently cherished him. In a very real sense, her beloved is her other self, her soulmate, bone of her bone and flesh of her flesh. In love, the two become one.

Love not only creates a union, but it also recreates each of the lovers who compose that union. It draws dormant traits out of them and refines some of their more obvious characteristics. In the Song, the woman is bold where she might never have been, and the man becomes the object and not merely the subject of desire and searching. The absences to which the poems allude require that the yearning lovers be patient and wait for the time of their reunion. The nature of their love instills within them a fidelity that neither separation nor discouragement can undermine. Furthermore, love seems to make a poet of everyone. At least it is true in this case, for both the woman and the man are lyrical as they sing the praises of the other. Love fashions eyes that see deeply into the heart and there discover goodness and grace too often hidden from the view of others. It heightens every sense, attuning one to the sights and sounds, the scents and sensations of the world.

Human love dissolves the defenses that we have built up to protect ourselves from harm. As we give ourselves to another and accept the gift of that other in return, we become both trusting and trustworthy. The vulnerability that may have formerly frightened us can, in the embrace of mutual respect, be converted into unguarded and unpretentious openness. Love creates new communities of acceptance and respect.

As dependent as we are on each other, as important as social compliance might be, there is still a way in which we stand alone before God. Ultimately, maturity requires that we alone make some of the major decisions in our lives, that we be true to ourselves in our particular circumstances. This means that we must understand these circumstances, but we must also know and appreciate our own uniqueness. It is only as responsible individuals that we can be effective companions.

Our desire for passionate union with another was placed deep within our being by the Creator. We long for kindred spirits, for hearts that are open to us, for arms that will embrace us. We come from the womb of another, and we are not at home without the assurance of some form of human intimacy. No one has to tell us that it is not good for us to be alone. We know this instinctively, and so we yearn for union with another.

Secondly, the nature-sensitive quality of these poems is extraordinary. In the memories of both the woman and the man, there are fragments of sight, smell, taste and touch, and from these imagery is fashioned that describes the respective lover. The exuberance of a spirited mare and the extravagant trappings that adorn it create a lasting mental image of vivacity and flamboyance. The delicacy perceived in a dove resonates with a tender chord in the human heart. The early growth of the woodland floor, first-green and sweet-smelling in its innocence, inundate the senses, as do the towering and aromatic trees. The forest carpet gently cushions the lovers. Both the rose and the lily modestly unfold their beauty and release their fragrant bouquet in the process. Pulp from the shrubs of the earth emit heady aromas that perfume the air and open the doors of the mind to exhilarating forms of consciousness. The fruits of the apple and of the vine tantalize the palate with refreshment and delight. The natural world paints its own portrait on human consciousness and provides the language for proclaiming love's beauty.

While it is true that metaphor is a poetic invention, there must be some kind of common ground that allows the comparison. That common ground is the natural world itself. In its various manifestations, it is vivacious and flamboyant, delicate and innocent; it is modest in its beauty, exhilarating in its many and varied fragrances; its touch is comforting and loving. Nature affects us as it does, because we are a part of it and it is a part of us.

We are born mature-mystics. As infants we are charmed by bright colors; as children we discover secret worlds in cloud formations; as young adults we are mesmerized by sounds; and as we grow in our appreciations, we are in awe of sunrises and sunsets. We instinctively turn toward the beauty of our world. In it we discover that for which our senses were made; we discover our common bond with nature. "And God saw that it was good."

Finally, although this unit has been identified as a dialogue between the lovers, its principal perspective is that of the woman. It is primarily her sexual interest and her longing that are featured, her beauty that is described. The character of this portrayal concurs with the contemporary image of a self-confident woman, one who is not embarrassed by her own sexuality or intimidated by the sexuality of the other. There is nothing vulgar about this expression of passionate desire. It is quite natural, and there is no hint that the poet thinks it is improper.

III

Love Sought and Found

The second unit (2:8–3:5) can easily be divided into two distinct parts: the woman's account of a verbal exchange between herself and the man (2:8-17) and her report of a search for and meeting with her beloved (3:1-5).

The Voice of love (2:8-17)

B   ⁸Hark! my lover—here he comes
    springing across the mountains,
    leaping across the hills.
  ⁹My lover is like a gazelle
    or a young stag.
Here he stands behind our wall,
    gazing through the windows,
    peering through the lattices.
  ¹⁰My lover speaks; he says to me,
    "Arise, my beloved, my beautiful one,
    and come!
  ¹¹"For see, the winter is past,
    the rains are over and gone.
  ¹²The flowers appear on the earth,
    the time of pruning the vines has come,
    and the song of the dove is heard in our land.
  ¹³The fig tree puts forth its figs,
    and the vines, in bloom, give forth fragrance.
Arise, my beloved, my beautiful one,
    and come!
  ¹⁴"O my dove in the clefts of the rock,

in the secret recesses of the cliff,
Let me see you,
 let me hear your voice,
For your voice is sweet,
 and you are lovely."

B ¹⁵Catch us the foxes, the little foxes
   that damage the vineyards;
    for our vineyards are in bloom!

   ¹⁶My lover belongs to me and I to him;
    he browses among the lilies.
   ¹⁷Until the day breathes cool and the shadows lengthen,
    roam, my lover,
   Like a gazelle or a young stag
    upon the mountains of Bether.

Several explanations of the structure of this first part have
been advanced. The repetition of words and refrains makes
the pattern difficult to determine. For example, reference to
the man as a gazelle in verses 2 and 17 form an *inclusio* (a
kind of parenthesis that begins and ends the same way), but
the obvious balance of verses 1 and 2 suggests that these two
verses belong together, thus calling for a modified notion of
inclusio. Verses 10 and 13 both end with the same phrase. It
is not clear whether this is a refrain or another *inclusio.* In the
face of this complexity, it seems that the best way to understand this part is as a composite of literary forms that are
interwoven throughout the speech.

 As already mentioned, verses 8 and 9 are carefully balanced descriptions of two moments in the approach of the
man. The Hebrew word with which verse 8 begins can be
translated as the noun "voice" or as an interjection "hark!"
Either version of the word fits the context of the segment.
However, while the words of the beloved are indeed recalled
(vv. 10-14), and the word itself has an auditory reference,
the structure of these verses (8-9) suggests that the word is

introductory, an exclamation that calls attention to what is about to occur. A second interjection, "here he comes," used with a participle indicates that the action is present: "Here he comes . . . here he stands." In her excitement at the approach of her beloved, the woman seems to exclaim: "Pay attention! Look, here he comes! Look, here he is!"

The man's approach is swift, full of anticipation. He comes leaping and bounding like a gazelle or a young stag (words carried over from the preceding adjuration where they appear in feminine form, v. 7). Upon his arrival, the forcefulness of his movement and of his sexual desire settles in his gaze as his eyes search for her. Intent on union, he calls out: "Arise and come." The verbs in this description of the man (referred to by the woman in each verse as *dôdî*) are all in couplets– leaping and bounding (v. 8); looking and gazing (v. 9); speaking and saying (v. 10)–all demonstrating the intensity of his fervor.

The *inclusio* that frames his words is tender yet urgent: "Arise, my beloved, my beautiful one, and come" (vv. 10, 13). "Beloved," one of his pet names for her (cf. 1:9, 2:2) is coupled with "beautiful one" (cf. 1:8), just as it was in an earlier poem (1:15). These epithets are evidence of his affection for the woman. The names themselves are loving and admiring. There is no suggestion of patronage or conde- scension. These and the corresponding names she has for him exemplify the mutual nature of their love.

Although he was fleet and decisive in coming to her, the man stops at the wall. Rather than entering the place where she is, he calls her out to meet him. First he comes to her; now she must go to him. There is mutual advance here, reciprocal assertiveness. It is not shyness that prevents his entrance; he has already demonstrated his own forcefulness and self-assur- ance. The text itself contains a series of motive clauses that explain why he summons her (v. 11). She is urged to come forth, just as the new life of spring has come forth.

What follows (vv. 11-13c) is a collage of images of nature's awakening at springtime, images that appeal to sight, sound and scent. Winter, the rainy season, is over and nature is coming alive anew. The profusion of vibrant wild flowers that cover the earth like a multicolored carpet, the sound of the migratory turtledove recently returned from its winter haven, the flow of sap through the fig tree ripening its fruits, the regeneration of vines as they bring forth blossoms and give forth fragrance are all harbingers of spring. It is into this burgeoning of spring that the man entreats his loved one to come. The delicacy of new life and the promise that it extends, the enchantment with which spring invades the senses, both evoke and mirror the splendor of their own passion. Calling the woman into spring is calling her into love.

Although his arrival has been swift, the man's advance has stopped short of union. In fact, the woman seems to be inaccessible to him, withdrawn like a dove hidden in the high crevices of a cliff (2:14). In an earlier poem he compared her eyes to those of this gentle bird (1:15). Here "dove" is another term of endearment that he uses to refer lovingly to the woman. It is an apt metaphor, for both the sight and the sound of the dove bespeak tenderness. The soft lines of the bird's contour and the purity of its color suggest gentleness; the sound of its cooing has a calming effect on the spirit.

Visual and auditory sensations are also the focus of the sentiments that follow this address of endearment. In a chiastically structured poem (v. 14), the man pleads to see the woman's lovely face and to hear her sweet voice. The longing for her presence and the pleasure that it brings spill over in these words of one consumed by love. This short poem is a fitting conclusion for a speech filled with allusions to sight and sound.

The woman responds (v. 15), picking up the themes of springtime and vineyard (vv. 11-13). Now her attention turns to a threat that the vineyard must face at this time of year. One of the predators against which the new season's young vines must be protected is the fox-cub. In its search for insects, this vivacious little animal burrows into the ground, laying bear the roots of the defenseless plant. For this reason, fox hunting is frequently a necessary occupational sporting event for vine dressers. The repetitive parallel structure of this verse suggests that it might have been some kind of a song or ditty that was popular during the spring fox hunt. Placed on the lips of the woman, it becomes a kind of teasing response to the man's plea to hear her voice. By using it, she is telling him that she does not want anything to threaten the well-being and the prospects of their love.

The report of this verbal exchange between the lovers ends with a declaration of the mutuality that characterizes their relationship: "My lover belongs to me and I to him" (cf. 6:2; 7:11 for slight variations). The phrase reiterates the attachment implied in the various terms of endearment used throughout the poems. He is hers: "my lover" (1:13, 14, 16; 2:3, 8, 9, 10); and she is his: "my love" (1:9, 15; 2:2, 10, 13); "my beautiful one" (2:13); "my dove" (2:14). The phrase actually epitomizes the entire collection of poems. The possessive pronouns imply reciprocal self-giving and acceptance of the other. The nature of this relationship is love. Every sentiment, every description in the Song of Songs flows from or exemplifies the reality described in this simple but profound declaration–He is mine, and I am his.

What follows this statement cannot be as easily understood as was the preceding segment. The scene is changed. The man was earlier portrayed as a shepherd, tending his herd in the fields along with the other shepherds (cf. 1:7f), but here his flocks graze among lilies and not in a pasture as one would expect. In a later poem he is portrayed as pasturing his flock in the gardens, among the lilies (6:2), and in yet another poem it is the gazelles, a metaphor for the woman, that feed among the lilies (4:5). All of this leads one to conclude that the lilies, among which the flocks are pastured, may be understood figuratively here as well. Such an interpretation corresponds to the other figurative references to lily throughout the Song. It is used as a metaphor for the woman (2:1f) and for the lips of the man (5:13). It also appears as part of a description of the woman's abdomen (7:3). The sexual undertones of such an interpretation cannot be denied. Lilies in some way refer to the charms of the woman, whether specifically to her lips (corresponding to 5:13), or generally to her overall appeal. The latter is most likely the intent in this unit.

If lilies are to be interpreted figuratively, then the pasturing of flocks should be understood in that way as well. The man has already been described as somehow engaged in this occupation (1:7f), and therefore it is quite appropriate to use pasturing as a metaphor of another activity that occupies his time and that requires his commitment. That occupation is lovemaking. When flocks are pastured, they are allowed to graze at will, to seek and to discover what will give them sustenance and pleasure. Although the shepherd allows the flock a certain amount of liberty in its meandering, such freedom of movement is only allowed within boundaries set by the shepherd, boundaries intended to protect the flock from straying out of reach or from being attacked by predators. In this poem, the woman first proclaims the devotion and union that she enjoys with her beloved, and then she describes their interaction using a figure of speech that has obvious erotic connotations.

The time of this encounter is daybreak, the time when the morning breeze rises and the night shadows recede (v. 17). Once again the meaning of the text is ambiguous. Is the woman asking the man to stay with her until daylight, to enjoy the pleasures of their love? Or is she urging him to flee before the light of day betrays his presence? Whichever the case, the text describes a romantic encounter between the woman and the man, an encounter that will eventually end, causing the lovers to part. Unlike the preceding segment, here it is the woman who invites and the man who must respond. This reversal of roles demonstrates how both of the lovers are in turn assertive and responsive.

The shift from third person descriptive to second person address is an example of the poetic device known as *enallage*, a device employed in the very first poem of the Song (1:2-4). The identification of the mountain (*beter*) is another point of uncertainty. Some commentators believe that it is the proper name of a specific mountain. Others contend that it is an allusion to the breasts of the woman. Still others consider it a reference to a spice-producing location. The parallel of this poem with another (4:5; cf. 8:14) suggests that the allusion is to spices rather than to some geographic designation or female attribute. Translating the word in this way is in keeping with the metaphorical character of the entire unit.

The Song of the Soul: There are several aspects of this reverie that might coincide with values that influence a contemporary spirituality. First there is the clear and unabashed erotic character of the relationship. Both the woman and the man use very sensuous language to speak of their mutual love and respective lover. The animals to which each compares the other are animals that possess qualities with distinct amorous connotations. The gazelle or young stag is known for its sexual prowess, and the dove is frequently characterized as a symbol of innocent romance. Plant life is also employed in this impassioned description. Since love poetry regularly compares the fecundity of the natural world with the fruitfulness that human love promises, the longing for union that pervades most of this poem is heightened, as nature image follows nature image in the description of the emergence of spring. The most erotic allusions are found in the final verses (vv. 16-17) where an intimate tryst is suggested and some type of union is proclaimed.

Although the sensuous portrayals are flamboyant in the imagery employed, it is clear that the behavior of the lovers

48

was in fact restrained. Though both were prompted by desire, the man was respectful of the circumstances of the woman's situation, and she in turn was protective of him. There is nothing in the portrayal that suggests anything shameful or illicit in this attachment, nor does the poet lead us to question the appropriateness of the lovers' infatuation. In fact, the opposite is true. This love develops virtue in both the woman and the man. It is passionate yet considerate. Though charged with the personal desire, it is not selfish. The erotic devotion has clearly brought out the best in both of the lovers.

The poem depicts mutual desire for and respect of the other. There is no gender domination in this relationship. The initial assertiveness of the man is far from oppressive or self-serving. There is no doubt about his eagerness to appease his yearning for the woman. The speed of his advance toward her is evidence of this. Still, he is respectful of her enclosure. He does not force his way in. Instead, he invites her out. She, on the other hand, responds positively to his words. Though in this instance she does not initiate the encounter, she is not the totally passive woman some gender stereotypes depict. Her own assertiveness is evident in the last part of this particular account where, presumably having invited the man to join her, she forthrightly orchestrates the duration of his stay and determines the time of his departure.

There is an ebb and flow in the mutually deferential assertiveness/responsiveness in this encounter. Neither partner is insensitive to nor minimized or frustrated by the other. For each of them, the tryst is an opportunity both to give love and to receive it. This complementary sensitivity could only be possible if both the woman and the man possessed a sense of her or his own personal value and desirability and was appreciative of the attractiveness and the inherent dignity of the other. Neither of them is a pawn for the exclusive pleasure of the other; they are both thoughtful sources of reciprocal delight.

49

Mutuality is not an easy quality to cultivate. It requires a different kind of balance than does equality. It seeks complementary involvement or reciprocal response. In a mutual relationship, one supplies what the other lacks. It is difficult to cultivate, because if our partner does not enter into the relationship as we do, we tend to think that he or she is not involved at all.

Mutuality requires that we respect and accept the otherness of our partner. Otherness sometimes seems alien to us. Because it is other, it can make us uncomfortable. Because it is other, its value is not always recognized. Because it is other, we may reject it as inadequate, and in rejecting it, we may be rejecting an expression of the love of the other.

In the mutual dance of love, sometimes we lead and sometimes we follow. With our partner, we hear the music and we feel the rhythm. As we come to know the body of the other in the dance, we learn to improvise the steps. Mutual love is improvisation sung by harmonizing voices. At times the musical intervals are close together, at other times they are far apart, but the harmony remains. Mutual love embraces the contrast of colors as well as their blending. It welcomes various shades and hues and creates a vibrant array of glory.

Mutual love is a highly prized gift given by one lover to the other. It is born in acceptance and it grows in the warmth of understanding and trust. It will only thrive if it is nurtured by both. When it is, it becomes the womb from which other love is born.

Finally, there is a remarkable nature-sensitive dimension to this portrayal. By its association with spring, the love is characterized as fresh and innocent and at the same time as sensuously appealing. There is an eagerness to savor its pleasures and a reserve before it that is respectful and demure. There is no contradiction in this representation. The passion displayed is chaste because it is faithful; it springs from the enchanting nature of the loved one and it seeks

50

union with that one alone. It is not overbearing or self-seeking; it is tender and considerate. This "love is patient . . . it is not rude, it does not seek its own interests . . ."

The poetry boasts several examples of familiar similes, where aspects of nature characterize human attributes. The enthusiasm of the man is analogous to the agility of the gazelle or young stag, and the charms of the woman compare to the gentleness of the dove. In these examples, the human attribute is the subject of attention, and the particular aspect of nature serves as an element of description. However, there is more in this poem than mere conventional poetic technique. Nature is not valued simply for its instrumental usefulness. It does not merely serve as a resource for poetic enthusiasm. The unusual portrayal of the birth of spring itself becomes the focus of attention here, and nature then becomes the model after which human love is called to pattern itself. The intrinsic value of the natural world is here recognized and acclaimed, and humans are invited to conform to nature's rhythms.

Although the poet is clearly captivated by the marvels of creation, the praises proclaimed should not be mistaken as nature idolatry. The mysterious forces of life and the breathtaking beauty of nature are not accorded divine properties. They are seen and revered for what they are, the marvels of the world of which the woman and man are a part. The poet is a nature-mystic not a worshipper of nature.

The Search For Love (3:1-5)

B   ¹On my bed at night I sought him
    whom my heart loves—
   I sought him but I did not find him.
  ²I will rise then and go about the city;
    in the streets and crossings I will seek
  Him whom my heart loves.
   I sought him but I did not find him.

³The watchmen came upon me
      as they made their rounds of the city:
      Have you seen him whom my heart loves?
   ⁴I had hardly left them
      when I found him whom my heart loves.
   I took hold of him and would not let him go
      till I should bring him to the home of my mother,
      to the room of my parent.
   ⁵I adjure you, daughters of Jerusalem,
      by the gazelles and hinds of the field,
   Do not arouse, do not stir up love
      before its own time.

The second part of this unit (3:1-5) describes the woman's yearning for the man she loves (vv. 1-2b), her search for him (vv. 2c-3), and her eventual discovery of and union with him (v. 4). It depicts once again the theme that runs throughout the entire book, that is, seeking and finding the loved one. Because of its similarity to a dream sequence in a later poem (5:2-8), some commentators maintain that this poem is also the report of a dream. Others consider it a daydream, a reverie or romantic fantasy. However, there is nothing in the poem itself to suggest either of these interpretations. Despite some of the uncharacteristic behavior of the woman described in the poem, it sounds like an account of an actual event. Her desire and the determination with which she seeks satisfaction of this desire is not new (cf. 1:7). Fearlessly she sets out in search of the man she loves.

The poem possesses an internal consistency created by the repetition of a word or phrase from one verse to the next. This literary linking begins with the previous unit. The nocturnal setting described there (2:16f) is carried into this poem (v. 1); the search for "him whom my soul (heart, cf. p. 27) loves" (v. 1) becomes almost a refrain (vv. 2, 3, 4; cf. 1:7a); the woman goes into the city to find the man (v. 2), but there in the city she is found by the sentinels (v. 3) before she finds him, presumably, in the city as well (v. 4). The

52

interplay between union (2:16f) and separation (3:1-3) and union again (v. 4) is characteristic of the entire book. On the one hand, this seeking and finding creates the book's dynamic expectancy. On the other hand, it is what leads many to consider it a collection of unrelated poems. Finally, the adjuration with which this unit ends is a repetition of the directives given to the daughters of Jerusalem at the end of an earlier poem (2:7).

The scene opens with the woman lying on her bed and, as is the case night after night, longing for the presence of her beloved. Her yearning will not be assuaged, nor will she sit passively, waiting for him to come to her. Instead, she will go into the city in search of him. Although the city is not a place for women, certainly not respectable women, the behavior of this woman is reminiscent of Woman Wisdom who also went alone into the city in search of men whom she loved (cf. Prv 1:20f; 8:1-3).

Her efforts in the city are futile. As she had on her bed in her own room, she sought him in the city but did not find him (vv. 1-2). However, in the city she herself is found by the sentinels as they are making their rounds. Her presence in the city is unusual for several reasons. First, in patriarchal societies the city was the domain of men, not women. Second, when women did venture forth, they were in the presence of a guardian man, not unaccompanied. Third, if such a situation ever did occur, it would have taken place in daylight, not at night. Finally, women did not initiate conversation with men, especially men with whom they were not acquainted.

Obsessed with longing, the woman defies social propriety and ignores possible societal denunciation. One concern occupies her: "Where is the one whom my soul loves?" In this poem, the sentinels make no reply. This should not be any surprise, because the poem is really not about them. There is no indication that they question her presence in the city, alone and at night, or her bold approach to them and her unabashed inquiry. They play no significant role other than to point out the force and extent of the woman's longing for the man. She will risk everything to find him. The fact that she continues her search after having encountered them (v. 4) is further evidence of this.

It is interesting to note the various settings within the Song that were possible or actual places of rendezvous. There are invitations to meet in the pasture (1:7f), in a flowering grove (2:10-13), and now the hope is for an encounter in the city (3:2f). Each of these places is somehow circumscribed. Pastures were probably the most open areas, but they usually did have certain boundaries. The same is true of groves. They may not have been fenced in, but the density of their growth provided them with natural borders. Finally, the city was the most confined, walled as it was for defense. The places of rendezvous did offer some degree of enclosure.

All of these places afforded men a kind of easy access that was customarily denied women. In addition to this aspect of discrimination, in several of the encounters mentioned there appears to be a certain degree of social disapproval of the woman's circumstances. Her exposure to the sun while in the pasture and her presence in the city alone at night appear to be questionable (1:6f; 3:2f [cf. 5:7]). The tryst in the grove has its own challenges. The departure of the man is orchestrated so that the clandestine nature of the meeting is safeguarded (2:16f). Since the comings and goings of men were seldom questioned, this caution had to be for the sake of the woman.

Despite the risks involved, in none of these cases is the woman deterred by possible social disapproval. Her longing for the presence of the man she loves prompts her to disregard whatever might keep them apart. Motivated by love, she ignores social protocol and risks the criticism that might come with detection.

Throughout the poems, whenever the lovers are finally united this event comes about without the aid of others. This is certainly the case here. With no help from the sentinels, the woman finds the man she loves (v. 4). She finds him; she clings to him; and she brings him into the house of her mother. Others may try to keep the lovers apart, but longing and the intensity of their ardor overcome any obstacles. The lovers meet and rejoice in their mutual embrace.

This is not the first-mention of the loving union of the couple. The first is merely an allusion. No specific embrace is described, but the erotic intentions of the man in bringing the woman into his chamber are obvious (1:4). The second suggests a room that contains a couch upon which they lie in each other's arms enjoying the delights of lovemaking (1:12). The third mentions a banqueting house within which the couple prepare for making love (2:4). The site of the next encounter is not clearly identified, but the amorous nature of the meeting is quite clear (2:16f). Finally, the woman brings her beloved into the house of her mother, the very place where she herself had been conceived (cf. Gn 24:28; Ru 1:8). The sexual connotations are unmistakable.

This last verse creates a kind of *inclusio*. At the beginning of the poem the woman is on her bed, presumably in her room (in her mother's house?). Spurred on by love, she leaves the security of this enclosure and risks the dangers of the outside world. Upon finding her beloved, she returns with him to the safety of her mother's house, into the room of her conception. Just as there is a constant interplay between seeking and finding, so there is movement from inside to outside. This not only symbolizes the shift of emotion that accompanies impassioned love, but it sustains the fast movement within the Song of Songs itself.

The adjuration addressed to the daughters of Jerusalem (v. 5) is identical to one that follows an earlier description of an amorous embrace (cf. 2:7). As with this earlier encounter, the daughters are asked to refrain from arousing love, a request that is difficult to understand considering the circumstances described in the poem. It insists that the movement of love be undisturbed and be allowed to follow its own course. However

55

this request fits within the thought of the respective poems, in each instance the adjuration signals the conclusion of a unit.

The Song of the Soul: The character of this entire segment corresponds well with values that influence a contemporary spirituality. The poem describes the wholesome passion of the woman, the heartfelt tenacity of her search for the man she loves, her undaunted courage in overcoming all possible obstacles, and her confident assertiveness in directing the circumstances of the couple's meeting. These are all virtues necessary for mature behavior in any situation. They are undoubtedly important in a relationship of mutual self-giving and trust.

The wholesomeness of the passion in human love is implicit in the writings of several of Israel's prophets. The metaphors of bride and bridegroom are used by Hosea (2:14-16), Isaiah (54:4-8; 62:1-5) and Jeremiah (31:31-34) to symbolize the covenantal love that Israel's God had for the people. Such language would never have been chosen if anything about its passion had been held suspect. It should be noted, that the point of this metaphor is God's love for the people, not their commitment to God. If human love is a fitting way of characterizing divine love, then human passion itself is undeniably a praiseworthy attribute.

Tenacity in one's commitment to love is another covenant virtue. In fact, steadfast love is the foremost characteristic of covenant allegiance (cf. Ex 34:6f; Nm 14:18; Pss 5:7; 33:5; 59:17; 89:28; 136:1-26; 145:8). Once again, this is a virtue that characterizes God's commitment, not Israel's. The Old Testament records account after account of God's steadfastness, even aggressive determination, despite Israel' fickleness. Nothing seems to have deterred God from this love. If such tenacity is appropriate for God, it is certainly an attribute to be admired in this woman.

Closely allied to tenacity in one's commitment is the virtue

56

of courage, that characteristic which enables one to brave any and all obstacles or setbacks in order to attain one's goals. The woman has certainly exhibited this quality, placing herself in both physical and social jeopardy, risking injury and reproach. Her willingness to suffer the consequences of her actions demonstrates how far above her own comfort she places her love. As God was never deterred by the limitations, weaknesses and faithlessness of Israel, so the woman is undaunted in her commitment to her love.

This same courage enables her to act assertively in pursuing the union that both of the lovers desire. She does not allow social convention to prevent her from seeking what she believes will be beneficial for both of them. Taking hold of life with all of its possibilities, choosing life rather than death (Dt 30:19) is a challenge that she embraces. There is no lack of confidence here. Convinced of the appropriateness of the course she and her beloved have set for themselves, she withstands all opposition. This poem sets forth a portrait of a woman of extraordinary virtue.

Love, whether of others or of God, often calls forth a tenacity and a courage that can surprise even the one doing the loving. Something happens when we are drawn to others in love, something that binds us to them. The threads of our separate lives intertwine and we are knit together. When this occurs, tenacity and courage are less attitudes that we choose than attitudes that choose us. They become natural responses to the new reality known as "us."

When we are tenacious in love, we cling not merely to our beloved but also to the "us" that we two have become. To relinquish our hold on this "us" is to diminish our new selves. Hardship might test the meddle of this new dimension of our being. As we face any possible hardship, we have no guarantee that our love will be strengthened rather than undermined. This is where courage comes in. Real love can call it forth; real love can even forge it. Love, whether of others or of God, is this powerful, this creative.

IV

Love's Extravagance

The third unit (3:6–5:1) is a mixture of poetic forms and images. It begins with an exclamation of wonder (v. 6), followed by a poem describing the extravagance of Solomon's royal furniture (vv. 7-11). It is difficult to attribute this account to any particular voice. Following this are two poems attributed to the man: a *wasf*, a type of Arabic poem that celebrates the beauty of the human body (4:1-7); and a second poem of admiration (4:8-15). Finally, there is a short exchange between the woman and the man (4:16–5:1).

Out of the Wilderness (3:6)

D   ⁶What is this coming up from the desert,
          like a column of smoke
     Laden with myrrh, with frankincense,
          and with the perfume of every exotic dust?

An unidentified speaker inquires: "What is this coming up from the wilderness?" The specific references to the column of smoke set the context for associating the wilderness mentioned here with the wilderness experience of ancient Israel. However, the word itself can refer to any uninhabited locale, and its meaning here should not be limited to that specific geographic place. This advance out of the wilderness is also reminiscent of the merchants' caravans that traveled across the ancient world, frequently coming out of the deserts. The column of smoke may well refer to the smoke that emanated from the burning myrrh, frankincense and fragrant powders, some of the exotic goods procured through such trade.

Spices further bring to mind the story of the queen of Sheba, who brought spices to Solomon and who, no doubt, was herself generously scented (1 Kgs 10:10). Although this initial exclamation may contain allusions to Israel's story as well as to the familiar experience of ancient traders in aromatic goods, the exclamation itself is probably nothing more than an exaggerated account of the approach of the litter. The royal connotations merely enhance the regal characterization of the couple.

The Royal Furniture (3:7-11)

[7] Ah, it is the litter of Solomon;
    sixty valiant men surround it,
    of the valiant men of Israel:
[8] All of them expert with the sword,
    skilled in battle,
Each with his sword at his side
    against danger in the watches of the night.

[9] King Solomon made himself a carriage
    of wood from Lebanon.
[10] He made its columns of silver,
    its roof of gold,
Its seat of purple cloth,
    its framework inlaid with ivory.
[11] Daughters of Jerusalem, come forth
    and look upon King Solomon
In the crown with which his mother has crowned him
    on the day of his marriage,
    on the day of the joy of his heart.

Several of the descriptive features of this part have led some commentators to classify it as the lyric that was sung at a royal wedding. In the first place, it is the only instance in the Song where Solomon is depicted as an actual character (vv. 7, 9, 11) and is not used as a standard of comparison (cf. 1:1, 5; 8:11-12). The poem also contains the only clear references in the Song to Israel (v. 7) or to Zion (v. 11). Finally, many of the allusions within the poem are not unlike those found in royal psalms (cf. Ps 45, an ode for a royal wedding).

While the poem may in fact have originated within royal circles and may even have been used during one of Solomon's many wedding celebrations (cf. 1 Kgs 11:1), its recontextualization within the Song of Songs indicates that the author/editor intended that it be understood within this new context. Here it furthers the metaphoric royal fiction of earlier poems. The references here need not be understood literally (cf. 1:4, 12), since the bride and groom of every wedding party were characterized, during the length of the festivities, as a royal couple.

The poem itself can be further divided into three segments. The first segment (vv. 7-8) describes the royal couch with its attendant honor guard; the second (vv. 9-10d) describes another piece of furniture; the third (vv. 10e-11) addresses the Daughters of Jerusalem/Zion. This is a very enigmatic poem. Not only does it introduce themes that are foreign to the character of the rest of the book, but its very composition appears somewhat contrived. Though the separate segments are distinct from each other, they seem to be deliberately related through references to Solomon and Israel/Zion. Finally, there are several Hebrew words that appear nowhere else in the Bible, making a precise interpretation of the entire poem difficult.

The word translated "litter" (v. 7) indicates that it was a portable piece of furniture, although there is no certain evidence in the passage that it was actually being carried here. What comes up from the wilderness is the woman. (This is contrary to a popular reading of the text, which sees v. 7 as the answer to the question posed in v. 6, the text thus yielding a depiction of a processional scene.) The exhortation "behold" is not followed by the verb form "it is" that would identify the approaching object as the "litter of Solomon." The exhortation itself merely calls attention to the litter and to the honor guard surrounding it.

Though arrayed for battle, the retinue of sixty mighty men have swords sheathed but not drawn, as would be the case in a situation of military alert. The dangers against which they stood most likely came not from some external enemy, but from nocturnal demons, "terrors of the night." The presence of these mighty men serves two purposes: They provide the honor due a royal figure; they act as a deterrent in the face of any possible danger. This interpretation fits well with the royal fiction found so frequently in wedding poetry. It was customary that the wedding couple be treated regally and be provided with an honor guard, who would, if necessary, aggressively oppose demons thought to threaten the newly married (cf. Tb 3:7f; 6:14f).

The precise classification of the second piece of furniture (vv. 9-10) is even more difficult to determine, since the Hebrew word that identifies it is found nowhere else in the Bible. This second piece of furniture was luxurious. Made of cedar from Lebanon, it was appointed with silver, gold and other costly materials. The appearance of several instances of words found in no other place in the Bible leaves many questions as to its actual construction, since the description itself fits both a portable and a stationary object. The silver posts that gave it security could be the poles used for carrying the sedan-chair or the pillars that formed the base of the throne. The gold spread that it boasts could be that upon which one reclined or an over-head canopy. The purple seat that added a dimension of royal dignity could be a cushion upon which to recline or upon which to sit. The meaning of the last phrase (v. 10d) is even more difficult to decipher.

The Hebrew word ordinarily translated as "love" can also mean "leather," which fits better in a description of a piece of furniture. One way of resolving the dilemma is to envision an elaborate leather interior, artistically decorated with romantic art, a feature that could be part of either portable or stationary furniture.

Here the daughters of Jerusalem are called on to witness the nuptial crowning of the king, a theme that suggests the union of the couple. Throughout the Song, these women appear as spectators to the love affair, rather than as active agents. Mention of them frequently follows an account of the couple's union (2:7; 3:5; 8:4). The other woman referred to is the mother of the king. This is the only time in the Song where she is mentioned and also the only time that marriage is actually noted. This mention and the connection between the two may stem from the original nuptial context of this poem. Although there is no textual evidence that a queen-mother actually crowned her son, her prominence in his realm is well known (cf. 1 Kgs 2:19; Prv 31:1-9). In the Song, just as the mother of the woman assisted in the love relationship (3:4; 8:2), so now does the mother of the man.

How then is this poem to be understood? In keeping with the overall movement of the Song, the woman and man experience the ebb and flow of absence, longing, presence, and absence again. The previous poem ended with the lovers in a passionate embrace (3:4). This poem presumes an absence, since the woman is portrayed as approaching. The desirability of each of the lovers is also a common theme throughout the Song. Here she is said to be richly perfumed, and he is characterized as a king with all of the resplendence and pageantry that attend royalty. These are themes that have appeared in earlier poems (cf. 1:4, 12). Finally, the daughters of Jerusalem stand as witnesses of the grandeur of this union. The woman has come out of the wilderness and, presumably, the man has met her with all of the splendor that is associated with a wedding.

The Song of the Soul: A contemporary spirituality would be quite interested in several features of the description provided in this poem. In the first place, the opulence depicted is an example of human dependence on natural elements. These elements are used either for making devices that ease human effort or for adorning human beings themselves with the splendor of the natural world. Both raw materials and their artistic reworking into human artifacts are products of nature without which life would be impossible.

Second, opulence also acts as an aphrodisiac. Here the heavy scents and fragrant powders perfume a litter that, in all probability, will serve as the bed for making love. It is only appropriate that this bed be made of priceless materials and be surrounded with intoxicating aromas. The honor guard heightens the importance of this litter.

Finally, although the primary focus of this scene is on the furniture of the man, the brief description of the woman's approach corresponds to certain ancient wedding customs wherein the woman proceeded from her own residence to the place which the man had provided for their conjugal union. Although it sounds like a patrilocal custom, one in which the woman goes to live with the man, she does not appear to be unduly restricted by this social custom.

Artistic ability is a God-given blessing. It is a mysterious eye that can see possibilities that the rest of us miss until they have been drawn forth. It knows what must be carved away in order that the sculpture can be born, what must be mixed so that the melody is released. Artistic ability shapes and embellishes; it fills and it balances; it joins the soul to the things of the earth and it raises it above them. It is no wonder that some have called it a touch of divinity.

A Vision of Loveliness (4:1-7)

G   ¹Ah, you are beautiful, my beloved,
        ah, you are beautiful!

63

Your eyes are doves
    behind your veil.
Your hair is like a flock of goats
    streaming down the mountains of Gilead.
[2] Your teeth are like a flock of ewes to be shorn,
    which come up from the washing,
All of them big with twins,
    none of them thin and barren.
[3] Your lips are like a scarlet strand;
    your mouth is lovely.
Your cheek is like a half-pomegranate
    behind your veil.

[4] Your neck is like David's tower
    girt with battlements;
A thousand bucklers hang upon it,
    all the shields of valiant men.
[5] Your breasts are like twin fawns,
    the young of a gazelle
    that browse among the lilies.
[6] Until the day breathes cool and the shadows lengthen,
    I will go to the mountain of myrrh,
    to the hill of incense.
[7] You are all-beautiful, my beloved,
    and there is no blemish in you.

The next part (4:1-7) is generally classified as a *wasf*, an Arabic poem that, with exaggerated metaphor and in an orderly fashion, describes the body of the loved one part by part. The imagery employed in such a poetic construction is normally taken from both nature and human craft. Most of the metaphors are visual allusions, but some of them appeal to other senses as well. While the imagery may seem strange, even crude to the modern reader, it must have been easily understood by the ancient Israelite and considered complimentary or it would not have become as popular as it was, nor would it have found its way into this collection of erotic poetry.

Most metaphors compare two largely unlike objects in an

attempt to elucidate the presence in one of them of a particular characteristic which they could share. For example: "Your eyes are doves" (4:1). Here, something about the doves is attributed to the eyes of the beloved. Some would say that the characeristic is the gentle quality of the bird/the beloved; others that it is the fluttering motion of the wings/the eyelids. The metaphor works, because the similarity is relatively easy to recognize.

The *wasf* may appear to be strange, even crude. However, there is another way of understanding metaphor based on emotional response rather than physical similarity. Viewed in this way, the metaphor "Your eyes are doves" generates a definite emotion. When it denotes the gentleness of the bird, it can create a sense of delicate calm. When the reference is to fluttering wings/eyelids, a tantalizing excitement is evoked. The *wasf* most likely grew out of the experience of being captivated by someone's physical charms, and it served as a way of arousing these emotions at a later time.

This particular poem begins and ends with a declaration by the man of the beauty of the woman he loves (vv. 1,7). The *inclusio* dictates how the various elements of description are to be understood. They all highlight one aspect of the remarkable beauty of her upper body. Her eyes, her hair, her teeth, her lips, her mouth, her cheeks, her neck and her breasts are all described. Despite the distinctiveness of the imagery used in this unusual form, several phrases found in other poems are also included (e.g. v. 1, cf. 1:15; v. 1b, cf. 6:5b; v. 6, cf. 2:17). It seems that the poet incorporated familiar poetic elements in order to integrate the unfamiliar *wasf* into this collection of erotic poetry.

The poem begins with an exclamation of admiration of the woman's beauty identical to one found in an earlier poem (cf. 1:15). However, in this instance an interesting phrase is added. Here the eyes are compared to doves looking out from behind a veil (cf. 2:14). The particular Hebrew word for veil is found only in the Song (4:1, 3; 6:7) and in Isaiah (47:2), making identification of the exact nature of the veil difficult to determine.

The veil is clearly unlike those that covered the entire head, concealing the identity of the wearer (cf. Gn 24:65; 38:14, 19), since the poem itself indicates that the woman's cascading hair can be clearly seen, and it becomes another object of the man's admiration. There is nothing in the text to suggest that this is a wedding veil, although the juxtaposition of this poem with the reference to Solomon's wedding in the previous poem has led some commentators to draw that conclusion. Others believe that this is a veil that covers much of the face, leaving the eyes visible. The veil is certainly intended for some degree of concealment. But is it concealment to hide or to beguile? If it is intended to cloak the attractiveness of the woman, the attempt is futile, for the eyes can be seen and their beauty captivates the man. The practice itself only accentuates the mysteriousness of the woman's eyes and makes them even more alluring.

This first metaphor clearly demonstrates the two ways that a metaphor can be understood. It is both descriptive and evocative. The engaging character of the woman's eyes is also seductive, capable of evoking an amorous response.

As already mentioned, the woman's hair is clearly seen. Its description as a flock of black goats presumably streaming down the mountainside suggests that it is cascading down her head, neck and shoulders. This image is dynamic not static. The undulating appearance of the moving flock suggests further that her hair is wavy. Unlike sheep that can be easily led, goats have been traditionally regarded as spirited, even unrestrained. Although this image applies to her hair and not to the maiden herself, hair has been associated with various human traits. Besides being a symbol of power (Samson) it can also imply unruliness (Ps 68:22; Dn 4:33). Even today, a woman's disheveled hair suggests that she herself is somehow unfettered by social protocol. This metaphor suggests that the locks of the maiden extolled here are both stunning and beguiling. While the metaphor captures a sense of the loveliness of her hair, the free-flowing buoyancy that it suggests creates a sense of excitement.

The image of a flock of goats is balanced with that of a flock of sheep (v. 2). As the former moved down the mountains in a energetic flow of black, this flock of sheep, coming up out of the water after having been washed in preparation for shearing, is a display of pure white wool. The straight white teeth of the woman resemble these sheep in their clean and ordered appearance. They are like twins, each upper tooth having a matching lower tooth. Scholars contend that twin births in sheep were very unusual in the ancient world. The poet may want to make the point that as unlikely as were twin births, so unusual was a full set of teeth. This metaphor adds another exceptional feature to the portrait of this extraordinarily beautiful woman.

The point about the woman's teeth also indicates something about the veil. This is a covering that allows both the tumbling hair and the woman's teeth to be seen. If this is a full face veil, it was made of diaphanous material which allowed the woman's entire face to be seen. This is certainly not a veil meant to completely conceal her features or the emotions reflected in them. The description of her teeth reveals something further about the woman. She would have to smile in order to expose them. To whom does she smile? Is her expression reserved for those of her intimate circle, or might she share her smile with anyone? There is nothing in the poems to suggest that she is a coquette, willing to grace everyone with the loveliness of her mouth. Therefore, the shape and color of her teeth is a feature about which only someone close to her would know. As with the metaphors that characterize her eyes and her hair, this metaphor both describes and evokes emotion. It describes the pleasing appearance of the woman's teeth, and it suggests the ability of her brilliant smile to enthrall those who behold it.

These first three metaphors, the dove, the flock of goats

and the flock of sheep, employ animal imagery taken from a rural pastoral setting. They all follow the same literary pattern: a part of the body is named; a comparison to it is made; the comparison is elaborated. A pattern of contrast can also be seen in the image of black and white flocks which stream down and come up respectively. These poetic details are testimony to careful literary artistry.

Having described the woman's attractive teeth, the man continues to extol the beauty of her mouth (v. 3). He is charmed by her lips, comparing them to a scarlet thread. Earlier her black hair suggested exotic abundance; her white teeth connoted purity. Here scarlet is a color that is associated with well-being and luxury (2 Sm 1:24). One would expect that her lips would be voluptuously full, but they are thin, like a thread. They would in fact be thin if she is smiling, as suggested above. In that case, as the smile spreads the lips across her face, it would also narrow their appearance. Finally, none of this could have been seen if the veil really concealed her face.

A slightly adjusted version of the literary pattern detected in the earlier metaphors is found here: The thread is described; the lips are named; the comparison is elaborated. Having described her lips, the man reflects on another feature of the mouth. The Hebrew word used here for mouth is found in no other place in the scriptures. It is a form of the verb "to speak," and it suggests that this exclamation of praise is here less focused on the shape and color of the woman's mouth than on its function as the organ of speech.

The man's preoccupation with the woman's face continues. The word for cheek comes from the word meaning "thin" and is found only in this description in the Song and in the story of Jael's murder of Sisera (Jgs 4:21f; 5:26). Jael is the woman who took a tent peg and thrust it through her enemy's temple. Most likely the word used refers to a part of the face where the bone is thin. The area referred to could be the upper cheek near the temple, close to the eyes. If, as the description of the woman indicates, the eyes are visible, this part of the face would be visible as well. On the other hand, if the veil is diaphanous, the woman's full cheek would be visible through the thin veil.

The woman's cheeks are compared to cut pomegranates. This plant, believed to be an aphrodisiac, has a blush-red color, a color that could be seen through a thin veil. This is actually an obscure metaphor that has been interpreted in several different ways. The reference could be to the cheek, to the forehead, or to the open palate. Although there is not agreement as to the part of the face meant, most scholars do believe that this is a reference to the color red. As with the other metaphors that comprise the *wasf*, this one is both vividly graphic and emotionally tantalizing. The description of the features of the woman's face and head begins and ends with the phrase "behind your veil" (vv. 1, 3). It seems that the veil, which is meant to cover her beauty, actually augments her mysteriousness, and this only serves to enhance her attractiveness, her inaccessibility, and her subsequent desirability.

The next detail of description (v. 4) is a comparison that is notably different from the preceding ones. The metaphor moves out of the category of natural phenomena into one that seems unflattering to contemporary Western sensitivities. Just as her neck, adorned with strings of jewels, was compared to that of a mare in Pharaoh's stables, here her neck is likened to a tower with military trappings. Unlike the previous nature imagery that celebrates the woman's delicate beauty, this image of a citadel bespeaks fearsome martial grandeur. The metaphor itself seems to be less interested in the length of the woman's neck than in the character of its adornment.

The word that reports the manner in which the tower was built appears no place else in the Bible, making an exact rendering of the phrase quite difficult. Most commentators believe that the allusion is to rows of masonry upon which

69

were hung military paraphernalia. The custom of hanging emblems of war from tower walls is well documented. This metaphor suggests that the reference intended is to a necklace consisting of several rows of ornamentation that graced the woman's neck. One might ask why this should be the image that resembles the embellished neck of this woman, who is otherwise characterized as being so beautiful. The answer may be found in the fact that standards of beauty can differ from culture to culture. In an Eastern culture, like the one depicted in the Song, the tower might symbolize regal stature, the trophies of victory would enhance its distinction. A metaphor that conveys such a meaning would not be judged inappropriate. Instead, it could be seen as both describing a feature of the woman's splendid appearance and inspiring awe in the face of such grandeur.

The final metaphor of the *wasf* (v. 5) returns to the pastoral setting with its use of nature imagery. The woman's breasts are compared to fawn twins of the gazelle, an animal renown for its grace and beauty. The very name of the animal comes from the Hebrew word meaning splendor or glory (cf. Is 4:2; 28:5). The precise point of the metaphor is obscure. It is unlikely that it is color, since a woman who would follow social custom and veil her face would hardly display her breasts so that their color would be clearly seen. "Twins" suggests symmetry, as was the case with the description of the teeth, and "fawns" suggests a youthful body and all of the comeliness that accompanies it. The praise of the woman's breasts is probably directed toward their firmness and shapeliness, characteristics which by themselves can inspire admiration.

The metaphor ends with what appears to be a kind of refrain: "that browse among the lilies" (cf. 2:16; 6:3). The similarities between this ending (4:5c-6) and an earlier one (2:16b-17) are unmistakable. In the first poem, it is the man who speaks; in this second poem, it is the woman. In each case, the other lover is somehow characterized as a gazelle and as feeding among the lilies. Although lilies are frequently symbols of fertility, in the Song they normally refer to some attribute of the woman (cf. 2:1f; by implication 2:16; 6:2f; 7:2; an exception is the reference to the lips of the man in 5:13). The metaphor itself is both graphic and evocative.

In addition to the mention of gazelles and lilies, the two passages (2:16b-17 and 4:5c-6) share two other features. They both contain the identical reference to the time of day ("until the day breathes cool and the shadows lengthen") and an allusion to mountains. In the first poem, the woman invites her beloved to savor their love until the light of day; in the second passage, the man declares that at that same time of day he will hasten to a place of exotic pleasure. The frankincense and myrrh are the same aromatic spices that perfumed the column of smoke, the allusion to the approach of the woman (cf. 3:6). All of these references suggest that the allusion is to the intoxication of lovemaking, whether actual or anticipated (cf. 1:13; 4:14; 5:1, 5, 13).

The *wasf* ends as it began, with a declaration by the man of the comeliness of his love (v. 1, 7). She more than measures up to the prevailing standards of beauty; she is flawless (v. 7b). Throughout the poem, the man has extolled several of her physical features, features that contribute to her sexual attractiveness. He has used imagery from both pastoral and urban settings (the slopes of Gilead, the tower of David), and he has compared her to animals that are both domesticated (goats and sheep) and undomesticated (doves and gazelle). Mention of his hastening to the mountains suggests his desire for union, not the realization of it. He is calling her to join him; they are not yet united. This song of admiration is clearly a song of yearning, a trait so characteristic of the Song.

The Song of the Soul: This understanding of the *wasf* harmonizes well with values found in a contemporary spirituality in each of the areas under consideration in this study. In the first place, its metaphors reflect a sensitivity to the integrity of creation. Then, it offers insight into the strength of the sensual allusions generated by these metaphors, insight that reflects an appreciation for human sexuality. Finally, it provides a dynamic portrayal of a vibrant woman, a portrayal sketched in the contours of a particular time yet open to legitimate contemporary reinterpretation.

It is clear that the poet who formulated this *wasf* was a keen observer of the world of nature. Most of the metaphors employed contain imagery that captures a notable trait of some specific animal. Recognizable yet frequently overlooked characteristics of the doves, the goats, the sheep and the fawns have here become proverbial and have been analogously applied to the object of the man's affection. The gentle fluttering of doves' wings, the rippling waves of black goats, the orderly procession of white sheep, the firm contours of twin fawns are, on the one hand, unremarkable natural phenomena. On the other hand, this resourceful poet has recognized the unique beauty in these phenomena and has recreated it into artistic representations of female comeliness.

Although the poet does indeed use images as media of description, it is an aspect of their natural form or behavior of the subjects and not their usefulness to humankind that is the point of comparison. Furthermore, the fact that these images are used to describe the extraordinary appeal of the man's beloved is clear evidence of the extent to which both the man in the poem and the poet recognize and value the beauty of these same natural phenomena. Finally, metaphors operate both ways. While attention is first on the woman's eyes that are likened to doves, soon it's the doves that call to mind the eyes of the woman. Nature is a vehicle for describing a human characteristic, and then the human trait becomes the vehicle for describing some feature in nature. The *wasf* is undeniable proof of the nature-sensitive character of this poetry.

The emotional responses evoked by the metaphors in this *wasf* are all highly erotic. The intensity of a fixed look, which can capture the eye of another and hold that person under a spell without making a move or speaking a word, and the fluttering movement of eyelids, which can also exert a mesmerizing influence over another, are not only engaging but also seductive. The sense of mystery that such eyes are able to cast can be accentuated if they are partially concealed behind a veil. Rippling black hair cascading down a woman's shoulders is not only attractive, it can also be quite suggestive. The woman's warm smile and her pleasant manner of speech imply a certain degree of intimacy. The color of her cheeks and the ornamentation around her neck both tantalize and inspire awe. The description of her firm shapely breasts is probably the most provocative image of all. The sensuality here is undeniable.

The man unabashedly uses these sensual figures of speech in his praise of the beauty of his beloved. The visual imagery is robust, and the movement depicted is energetic. Despite this, there is not even a hint of disapproval. One never gets the sense that he is considered too graphic in his portrayal, or that he is describing physical characteristics that should not be discussed. He is censored neither by the poet nor by anyone within the poem itself. On the contrary, both the subject of the characterization and the sensuousness of the imagery are in keeping with the nature of the rest of the poetry. The sexual attractiveness of the woman and the erotic attraction of the man are as natural as the nature-sensitive comparisons that comprise the poem. The very use of this particular literary form of praise (the *wasf*) shows that the sexual nature of their relationship is highly esteemed.

There is a very thin line between flirtation and sexual manipulation, making it very difficult to discern the role that physical attraction plays in human relationships. People today are quite critical of any exaggerated concentration on female beauty, concentration that reinforces biased stereotypes and minimizes other dimensions of a woman. They reject characterizations of women that serve purely chauvinistic objectives. They maintain that women must be valued for themselves and not merely for what they can contribute to the male ego, pleasure or comfort.

In many ways, the woman described in this *wasf* would be favorably regarded today. Although the man is clearly preoccupied with her beauty, he does not have control of it. He admires it, but he does not possess it. Her beauty is behind a veil, and even he seems to respect that. It is clear that she is the one who decides the course of action. The rest of the poetry of the Song shows that she is not playing the coquette. Instead, she is self-possessed and self-directed. Her use of the veil here may be nothing more than social custom.

There is a way in which the character and quality of our human commitments can act as a gauge for measuring the character and quality of our commitment to God. This is the case for two reasons. First, we engage the same aspects of ourselves in all of our commitments regardless of their diversity. The difference is in the value that we give them and in the degree of the intensity of our involvement. Second, from an incarnational point of view, it is often in our commitments to others that we commit ourselves to God.

A Garden of Delight (4:8-5:1)

8 Come from Lebanon, my bride,
  come from Lebanon, come!
Descend from the top of Amana,
  from the top of Senir and Hermon,
From the haunts of lions,
  from the leopards' mountains.
9 You have ravished my heart, my sister, my bride;
  you have ravished my heart with one glance of your eyes,
  with one bead of your necklace.

¹⁰How beautiful is your love, my sister, my bride,
how much more delightful is your love than wine,
and the fragrance of your ointments than all spices!
¹¹Your lips drip honey, my bride,
sweetmeats and milk are under your tongue;
And the fragrance of your garments
is the fragrance of Lebanon.

G ¹²You are an enclosed garden, my sister, my bride,
an enclosed garden, a fountain sealed.
¹³You are a park that puts forth pomegranates,
with all choice fruits;
¹⁴Nard and saffron, calamus and cinnamon,
with all kinds of incense;
Myrrh and aloes,
with all the finest spices.
¹⁵You are a garden fountain, a well of water
flowing fresh from Lebanon.
¹⁶Arise, north wind! Come, south wind!
blow upon my garden
that its perfumes may spread abroad.

B Let my lover come to his garden
and eat its choice fruits.

G ⁵:¹I have come to my garden, my sister, my bride;
I gather my myrrh and my spices,
I eat my honey and my sweetmeats,
I drink my wine and my milk.

B Eat, friends; drink! Drink freely of love!

The last two segments of this part, the song of admiration
by the man (4:8-15) and the short exchange between the
woman and the man (4:16–5:1), seem to be woven together
by means of a play on sound and the repetition of words. For
example, Lebanon (vv. 8, 11, 15) echoes the sound of the
Hebrew for frankincense, and in Hebrew the word for spice
(vv. 10, 14) sounds like that of fragrance (v. 16). Themes

that are repeated include honey and milk (4:11; 5:1), bride (4:8, 9, 10, 11, 12; 5:1) and garden (4:12, 15, 16; 5:1), to name but a few. This sensuous imagery appeals to sight, smell and taste. Such appeal is a fitting tribute to the intoxicating effects of love.

In many instances, the individual poems in the Song begin with the lovers separated from each other (cf. 2:8; 3:1; 3:6). This particular poem follows that pattern. It opens with a summons from the man, calling the woman to be with him (cf. 2:10-14). Earlier allusions to mountains (4:6) are taken up again in the references to Hermon, Amana and Senir (the Amorite name for Hermon), all peaks in the Anti-Lebanon range of the Lebanon Mountains. These majestic summits were known not only for their pristine beauty but also because they appeared to be unapproachable. The fact that this forested range was infested with lions and leopards added to the danger that it represented. These references are probably not to real geography, but are intended as figurative allusions to the general inaccessibility of the woman (analogous to the reference to clefts in the rock and recesses in the cliff; cf. 2:14).

This is the only poem in the Song where the man calls his love "bride," a name used here as a term of endearment and not as an identification of marital status. Another pet name frequently found in love poetry is "sister." The sibling relatedness is also understood figuratively, connoting physical intimacy not of kinship but of passionate love. The word "bride" divides the rest of the poem into two literary segments: Verses 8 and 11, along with "Lebanon," forms an *inclusio*; verses 4:12 and 5:1, "sister-bride" and "garden" forms a second *inclusio*. The entire segment (4:8–5:1) is replete with imagery that is very suggestive of passionate lovemaking.

The woman in the poem, affectionately called sister-bride, has such power over the man that he is beyond his senses (v. 9). In Hebrew thought, the heart is more the seat of understanding and discernment than emotion, as is the case in modern thought. Therefore, to say that she has ravished his heart is to say that she has driven him crazy, not unlike the way he has affected her (faint with love; cf. 2:5; 5:8). The explanation for his state of mind is given in a parallel construction that likens a power of a glance of her eye to that of a pendant on the necklace she is wearing. Her eyes, earlier compared to doves (1:15; 4:1), possess a calm beauty that is overpowering. Likewise, only one charm on her extravagant necklace (1:10; 4:4) is needed to entrance him. Since he has lost control of his senses, the smallest thing can cast a spell on him—a mere glance or a single accessory.

The love of this sister-bride not only dazzles his mind but inundates his senses as well. Its beauty gives much more pleasure than the pleasing bouquet and intoxicating qualities attributed to wine. He is also overcome by the fragrance of the oils that she uses to anoint herself. Their essence outclasses the scents of even the most exotic spices that are brought from afar. The man luxuriates in the delight that he takes in his love, and he describes the enchantment that he experiences, using exactly the same words as the woman used to acclaim the incomparability of the love that he has for her (1:2b-3a).

The poem continues the idea of sweetness. A parallelism juxtaposes her lips and her tongue and, using two synonyms for honey, describes the sweetness of each. The first synonym refers to the kind of honey that, because of its abundance, drips of its own accord from the honeycomb. In like manner, her lips drip of this honey. The second word identifies honey that is produced from date-syrup or grape-syrup or is harvested from the comb of the bee. Coupled with milk, this latter type is part of the standard phrase (milk and honey) that characterizes the fruitfulness of the promised land (cf. Ex 3:8; Lv 20:24; Nm 16:14; Dt 26:15; Jos 5:6; etc.). This honey is found under her tongue. Together these two references to honey suggest that the woman's mouth is overflowing with delectability, and that this delectability is both spontaneous and cultivated.

The parallel construction describing her mouth both augments the sensuous character of the imagery and allows the verse to be interpreted in two ways, either as a metaphor for her enticing speech (cf. Prv 5:3; 16:24), or as a description of her passionate kisses (cf. 5:13). Actually, either interpretation corresponds to the sense of the poem, and so one need not be chosen to the exclusion of the other. The very erotic picture alluded to in the next phrase seems to favor the second understanding. It marvels at the smell of her garments, a smell that matches the fragrances of Lebanon. The clothing referred to is the outer garment that was used as a cloak during the day and as a cover for sleeping at night (Dt 24:13). This sensuous description (vv. 9-11), which appeals to sight and taste and scent, concludes with a vague allusion to the woman's bed, the place where love can finally be realized.

The second segment (4:12–5:1) develops the garden motif (vv. 12, 15, 16; 5:1). While the Lover frequently breaks into praise, comparing his Beloved to a mare among the chariots of Pharaoh (1, 9), a lily among thorns (2, 2), a dove (2, 14), a palm tree (7, 8), or likening her eyes, hair, mouth, cheeks, neck and breasts to various animals, fruits, or objects of beauty (cf. 4, 1-5; 7, 2-6), none of these brief similes can compare with the strength and complexity of this unique passage. Part of this complexity is the dual meaning of garden, a metaphor which refers to the woman herself and to a place of rendezvous for the couple.

A pattern is found in all of the earlier verses of this segment (4:8, 9, 10, 12). The designation "bride" or "sister-bride" is preceded and followed by the same or a similar phrase. The recurring pattern has prompted an alteration of the text (v. 12). The Hebrew for "heap" or "wave" (*gal*) is amended to read "garden" (*gan*). The verse now conforms to the literary pattern and the reading yields two quite distinct images, a garden and a fountain. Even without the elaborate descriptions that follow, both of these themes suggest fruitfulness and abundance of life. An added detail cannot be overlooked: Both metaphors include a straightforward indication of deliberate enclosure. The garden is locked, allowing entrance to nothing and to no one; the fountain is sealed, preventing anything or anyone from withdrawing water.

These motifs are metaphoric, not descriptive; both the garden and the fountain refer to the woman. It is she who is enclosed. The passive participles suggest that the locking and the sealing have been done by another. However, the poetic nature of the metaphors discourage a literal reading of them. Who, if not the woman, would have locked the garden and sealed the fountain? She is the one who both denies access to the delights within her and who reserves for herself the life-giving riches that she possesses. These metaphors may refer to her virginal state or to the discretion with which she shares herself (cf. Prv 5:15-17). Whichever is the case, she is not an open field, vulnerable to any trespasser; nor is she a public fountain from which anyone might drink. Once again, the general inaccessibility of the woman is featured.

The Hebrew word meaning "to send forth" (v. 13) appears no place else in the Bible. It has been variously translated as "sprouts" or "branches" (cf. Is 16:8), as "water courses" (cf. Neh 8:6) or as "watered fields." Whether the word refers to branches that are sent forth from the garden or to water that issues from the fountain, the final outcome is the same—an orchard overflowing with sumptuous and marvelous fruits.

The word for "orchard" is a loan word from the Persian. Although in the Hebrew Bible it is never applied to the Garden of Eden, the Septuagint, or Greek version, uses it in its translation of the Genesis story. It is also through the Greek that it came to refer to paradise. The Hebrew word appears in only two other places (Neh 2:8; Eccl 2:5), and in both cases it refers to a royal garden. This may have less to do with monarchy as such than with the opulence of the garden which, most likely, only the throne could afford. This unique garden produced the very finest fruits (vv. 13, 16; cf. Dt 33:13-16) and choice spices (v. 14).

The first-mentioned plant is the pomegranate, a fruit that is frequently associated with the tree of life and which was considered an aphrodisiac. The many seeds within it account for belief in its fruitfulness and life-giving powers. The rest of the list of the plants in the garden are known for their aromatic properties. They are: the fragrant henna with nard; the aromatic nard and saffron; the sweet-smelling cane and cinnamon; the intoxicating frankincense; and the heady myrrh and aloes. Most of these spices were not indigenous to the land but had to be imported from India, Arabia or China. This only added to their exotic mystique. When applied metaphorically, the rarity of the vegetation in the fantastic garden denotes the exceptional nature of the woman's beauty. She is an incomparable garden, graced with beauty that is rare and unmatched.

The segment ends with three images of refreshing water (v. 15), all in parallel construction. The first expression, "garden fountain," brings together the two major images of the segment (v. 12). Metaphorically, they describe the resplendence and the fruitfulness of the woman. Although she is in fact compared to only one garden, the reference here is actually to a source of water that can feed more than a single garden. The second allusion is to what was considered living water, a bubbling spring in a well rather than stagnant water stored in a cistern. The last image is of the fresh water obtained from melted snow that flows down from the Lebanon mountain range. Each one of these three images suggests fresh water that will always be in abundance. Both the garden and the fountain possess unbelievable magnificence and fecundity, apt metaphors for portraying the unparalleled splendor of the woman.

The man's paean of admiration is followed by an invocation by the woman herself. Her words indirectly confirm his flattering appraisal of her garden (her own person). It does indeed abound with exotic vegetation that gives off captivating fragrances. He is also correct in stating that enjoyment of these pleasures is not open to all; not even he claims the right of entry into the garden. Continuing the motif of the garden's fragrance, she calls on the winds to blow upon it, causing it to breathe forth its intoxicating bouquet. This suggests that she is prepared to share her charms. Her garden now becomes his garden, and he (*dôd*) is allowed to eat its choicest fruits (cf. v. 13). She had earlier described him as an apple tree under whose shadow she sat in delight and whose fruit sweetened her taste (2:3). The picture is here reversed. It is obvious that their enjoyment is mutual.

The sensual character of the imagery and the double entendres that they create are clear indications of the sexual nature of the invitation. Up to this point, the woman has been very discrete in guarding her garden, but now she is open to her beloved. This may suggest that her virginity is still intact, but that she is now ready to make love. In an earlier poem she admitted that she has not kept her vineyard (cf. 1:6), another metaphor for herself (cf. 8:12). It may be that she has kept herself for her beloved alone, but that together they have in fact enjoyed, in some intimate manner, the love that they share.

The last verse consists almost exclusively of themes that have been used in describing the woman—garden, sister-bride, myrrh, spice, honey, wine. However, the difference between their meaning in the two places is striking. Earlier they were attributes to admire; here they are delights to relish. The man responds to the woman's invitation, enters the garden that is now his, and indulges himself in its luxuriance, describing his experience in the same figurative language he employed earlier to characterize her (cf. 4:10-12).

The union of the two is further indicated by the double use of the possessive pronoun "my" in each of the four lines of the verse. This underscores the fact that the woman and everything that makes her appealing are now his. This should not be misconstrued as possession of one person by the other. Rather, it should be understood against the background of the phrase, "my lover belongs to me and I to him" (2:16), where it implies intimate union and mutual belonging. Union is further suggested: the enjoyment of smelling the fruits of the garden is now changed to the delight of consuming them, eating and drinking carrying clear sexual connotations (cf. Prv 5:15f).

This segment and the entire unit end with an invitation to eat and drink. The literary construction of the verse is difficult to decipher and so its exact meaning is unclear. The identity of the speaker is also quite ambiguous. The phrase itself may have originally been a part of a drinking song. The euphoric cry that it contains fits well here as a jubilant song, a sign of the culmination of love's desire and final satisfaction. Throughout the Song, lovemaking has been compared to the exhilaration brought on by wine. It seems only appropriate that here, at the end of an individual poem which is also the end of one of the six units of the collection, and at the very middle of the book itself, there is an exhortation to drink deeply of love, so deeply that one is intoxicated with it.

The Song of the Soul: Reading the first poem in this segment (4:8-11) with an eye to contemporary spirituality reveals its nature-sensitive character. As has been the case throughout all of the poems, the magnificent imagery is evidence of the poet's appreciation for and reliance upon the wonders of the natural world. The poetic allusions appearing here are dependent upon the sensory stimulation resulting from the sights, fragrances, flavors and other sensations of the world. Before the dignity and reserve of the woman can be compared with the grandeur and awesomeness of the mountains (v. 8), the mountains themselves must be the object of respectful contemplation. Wine must be savored and its inebriating properties relished before its effects can be called upon to describe the pleasing taste and intoxicating character of love. The fragrances of oil and spices and the sweetness of honey had to be experienced and enjoyed before they could be added to the store of figurative allusions. It was only after certain aspects of nature were appreciated for their intrinsic worth that their instrumental value as poetic images could be determined.

The garden that is described in the second segment (4:12–5:1) is lavish with luscious fruits and exotic spices. In addition to this, it contains a fountain that supplies it with life-giving water. The mythological allusions in this poem, specifically the garden (paradise) and the pomegranate (the fruit of the tree of life) enhance the image of the garden's fecundity and pleasure. The poet is well aware of the distinctive properties of this garden. As a real garden, it holds the secrets of life; as a symbol of the primordial garden, it holds the secrets of creation. Very few realities can be more highly prized.

In addition to its nature-sensitive quality, the poetry also exhibits a genuine appreciation of human sexuality. The call of the man to the woman (v. 8) is not merely a summons. It is an invitation to union. The movement present in this segment makes this quite clear. First he calls her (v. 8); then he describes her incredible yet inaccessible beauty (vv. 9-15). Next she invites him to enjoy her and the pleasure that she can give (v. 16); he accepts her invitation and revels in the delight that she provides (5:1). This movement describes the very dynamic of love: yearning for the absent beloved; praise of the beloved's charms; an invitation to pleasure; and the joys of union.

Erotic allusions abound in every verse of this poem. First, the man is under the woman's spell; he is intoxicated, driven crazy. Next, the language he uses in his portrayal of her is highly sensuous, and the implications of this depiction are clearly sexual. The pleasure derived from the fruits and spices mentioned is much more than simple gratification. It is a kind of satiety that not only appeases normal desire, but also transports one to a much higher dimension of satisfaction. This superabundance of enjoyment corresponds to the exceptional degree of pleasure that the woman can provide. As sexually nuanced as this description is, there is never any question about the propriety of the man's interest. The woman's appeal is overwhelming, and his response to it is fitting.

The human body, whether male or female, is one of nature's wonders. It not only mirrors many of the characteristics of material creation, but it also experiences them and reacts to them. It is through the body that we are engaged in the world and with each other. It is both the instrument upon which nature plays a magnificent rhapsody and the very melody that is played. A hint of the creativity of God can be discerned in this stunning creature. Is it any wonder that we are charmed by it? that we adorn it? Our individual body, unique to us, is our way of being.

The poem ends (5:1) with a declaration of consummation. The man's yearnings have been realized, his cravings have been assuaged. She has granted him access to her delights; he has taken pleasure in them. The poetry celebrates their enjoyment, but it does even more. It invites everyone to drink deeply at the fountain of intoxicating love. This is further evidence of the high esteem in which human sexuality is held. The poem portrays it not only as natural, but also as beautiful. It should be noted that the lovers are not warned about the overwhelming power that sexuality can wield. On the contrary, it is this very power that is extolled. Sexuality can open us to another, prompting us to share whoever we are and whatever we possess with the other. It can also draw us into the world of the other, then to marvel at the grace and beauty that we find.

Finally, the self-possession of the woman, suggested by the unapproachability of the mountains and the indiscriminate inaccessibility of the enclosed garden and the sealed fountain, is a trait that is highly prized today. It is important to note that she is not described as self-centeredly isolated. She is assuredly in relationship with the man, but she is not ruled by him. She is willing to share her riches, but she decides when and how and with whom this is to be done.

Mutuality is another quality insisted upon today. This is a quality that certainly characterizes the love described here. The man is ravished by the woman, and she is faint with love for him. This is not a one-sided affair where one person dominates the other and the interests of that dominant party are the only ones considered. This is a love relationship where the passion is reciprocal and the pursuits of both parties are addressed. If anything, it seems that in this poem the woman wields the more influence.

V

A Man Like No Other

The fourth unit (5:2–6:3) consists of an account of the woman's dream, which ends with an adjuration to the daughters of Jerusalem (5:2-8) and a dialogue between the daughters and the woman, wherein they pose questions about her beloved (5:9; 6:1) and she responds (5:10-16; 6:2f). As the previous unit focused on the beauty and desirability of the woman, this unit celebrates the incomparability of the man.

A Dream of Love (5:2-8)

B   ²I was sleeping, but my heart kept vigil;
    I heard my lover knocking:
  "Open to me, my sister, my beloved,
    my dove, my perfect one!
  For my head is wet with dew,
    my locks with the moisture of the night."
  ³I have taken off my robe,
    am I then to put it on?
  I have bathed my feet,
    am I then to soil them?

  ⁴My lover put his hand through the opening;
    my heart trembled within me,
    and I grew faint when he spoke.
  ⁵I rose to open to my lover,
    with my hands dripping myrrh:
  With my fingers dripping choice myrrh
    upon the fittings of the lock.

86

⁶I opened to my lover—
    but my lover had departed, gone.
I sought him but I did not find him;
    I called to him but he did not answer me.

The watchmen came upon me
    as they made their rounds of the city;
They struck me, and wounded me,
    and took my mantle from me,
    the guardians of the walls.
⁸I adjure you, daughter of Jerusalem,
    if you find my lover—
What shall you tell him?—
    that I am faint with love.

Most commentators maintain that this first part (5:2-8) is a description of either a dream or a dreamlike fantasy. It is reminiscent of an earlier poem (3:1-5). Both begin with the woman as she is prepared for nocturnal sleep. Both relate her venture into the city in search of her beloved and her encounter with the sentinels on duty there. Both end with an adjuration of the daughters of Jerusalem. The similarities notwithstanding, the poems are quite different from each other, as the commentary will show. Speaking in the third person, the woman here recounts the approach of her beloved, her delay in acting on his request for entrance, his retreat, and her subsequent search for him. The absence-presence-absence theme is clearly sketched.

The poem opens with an expressed contradiction between being asleep and being awake. The deliberate contrast in these verbs has resulted in ambiguity of meaning and subsequent differing interpretations. Is the woman really dreaming? Is she in a state of semi-wakefulness? Is she fantasizing? Nothing in what follows in the poem corresponds to the typical dream narrative. In fact, the description of the episode in the city is quite realistic, suggesting that it could have really happened. Probably the reference to sleep and wakefulness can be best understood as a poetic fiction that draws its images from both the world of dreams and the world of reality. Interpreting the phrase in this way recognizes the use of double entendre, while insisting on precise and consistent meaning diminishes the poetic force of the imagery.

As stated earlier, the heart is more the seat of thought than of emotion. Thus, the woman may be in some state of sleep, but her mind is awake. The participial form of the verbs indicates that both sleep and wakefulness are states of some duration, rather than brief moments. Consequently, one can say that this is not a picture of a sleeping woman, awakened by the man's knocking on the door or window. Instead, she is in repose and alert at the same time. For this reason, she is able to call attention to the approach of her beloved (*dôdî*), "Hark!" (cf. 2:8).

The Hebrew word rendered "knock" denotes a forceful pushing rather than a gentle tapping (cf. Gn 33:13; Jgs 19:22). Such forcefulness does not fit the context of this poem well, for ultimately the man does not force entrance. Perhaps the word exemplifies the energy of the loving desire itself. He is seeking entrance. His entreaty is straightforward, but its meaning is ambiguous; "Open to me." The word "open" is used three times in this part (5:2c, 5a, 6a), never with a direct object, but always with *dôdî* as the indirect object. To what does he seek entrance? her room? or the woman herself? In either interpretation, the erotic character of his request is obvious.

The names that the man uses in addressing the woman have become familiar epithets in the Song. Each one includes a possessive pronoun, suggesting the uniqueness of the couple's relationship. "My sister," which denotes permanent physical intimacy, has an added erotic connotation, having been linked with bride (4:9, 10, 12; 5:1). "My beloved," a reference to an intimate companion, is his most frequently used term of endearment (1:9, 15; 2:2, 10, 13; 4:1, 7; 6:4). "My dove" is a pet name that characterizes the beloved as the gentle bird associated with love itself (2:14). "My perfect one," a name derived from the Hebrew word meaning complete, suggests integrity and excellence. It could refer to her unblemished beauty or to her undivided commitment to him (cf. 6:9). The ambiguity allows for both understandings.

The parallel construction that follows is difficult to interpret. It contains the man's explanation for his earnest desire for admittance. His hair is soaked with the chilly dew of the night. This kind of whining complaint of the man and the following reluctance on the part of the woman (v. 3) do not easily fit the tone of the love poetry of the Song. However, an unusual form found in Egyptian poetry might throw light on the meaning of this unusual feature. It describes a young man standing outside a girl's house, longing to get inside and complaining because he is prevented from doing so.

Such a situation certainly describes two scenes found in the Song (2:10-14; 5:2b). In the former, the man is outside and invites his beloved to come out and join him. In this second episode, he is outside and entreats her to let him in. While the form itself corresponds to the theme of unfulfilled desire for union so common in the poems, the man's grumbling and the woman's apparent indifference do not. This may be an example of the limitations one faces when borrowing a form from another literary tradition. The borrowed form corresponds to some of the features of the second tradition, but not to all of them.

The woman's reply is in exact parallel form. This explains why two reasons are given for her hesitation in responding to his entreaty, reasons that are as flimsy as were his motives for asking entrance. However, the contents of her reply are puzzling. Throughout the poems she has craved his presence and the intimacy that it promised. Here her words suggest that she is not only procrastinating, she is actually considering forgoing a midnight rendezvous. Some interpreters understand her response as a playful tease. Others believe that, awakened from sleep, she is bleary-eyed and confused.

Her response conforms to the pattern described above of the young man standing outside. However, it can also be read as a double entendre. The garment of which she speaks was the kind worn next to the skin. She has put this off; she is naked. Describing herself as such to the man is certainly provocative. There is a second sexual allusion. Washing the dust from one's feet was a bedtime ritual. However, the phrase was also used as a euphemism for male genitals (cf. 2 Sm 11:8, 11; Ru 3:3-9; Is 7:20). The use of this literary form allows the poet to be sexually suggestive without being erotically explicit.

The man is not deterred by the woman's apparent rebuff. Instead, he attempts to open the door himself by inserting his hand into the latch hole from the outside. The Hebrew construction here is cryptic. The verb denotes forceful movement *toward* something, while the preposition means away *from*. This has led some interpreters to hold that the man is thrusting his hand into the hole, and others to maintain that he is withdrawing it. The word "hand" also has sexual connotations. It has been used to refer to a memorial pillar, clearly a phallic symbol (1 Sm 15:12; 2 Sm 18:18; Is 56:5). Sexual nuances are also evident in its use in other passages (cf. Is 57:8, 10).

The woman's reaction to his gesture is intense. Her innards, the seat of emotion, are profoundly stirred for him. The word for innards or bowels is sometimes used in parallel construction with womb (cf. Gn 25:23; Ps 71:6; Is 49:1), according it a sexual connotation. The double entendre is clear. The phrase can mean that she has been emotionally touched to the core of her being or that the experience is a sexual one. However, to suggest that this verse is actually describing coitus is to ignore the account that follows, where the woman proceeds to open to her beloved (v. 5). This latter action makes no sense if thrusting his hand implies genital penetration and her stirring is an orgasmic response. Once again, the description is poetic, intended to suggest rather than to recount.

The woman finally does rise to open to her lover (v. 5). The scene is portrayed with imagery that is quite sensuous. A parallel form is used to describe the woman's hands. They literally drip with myrrh as she opens the bolt of the door. Myrrh is not merely an aromatic resin. Within the Song it always has erotic connotation (1:13; 3:6; 4:6, 14; 5:1). Though the image of dripping myrrh is explicit, the origin of the myrrh is not. Did it come from the woman who, in preparation for a night of lovemaking, may have generously perfumed herself before retiring (cf. Prv 7:17)? Did it drop from the hand of the man when he thrust it through the latch hole in an effort to gain access to the woman?

On the other hand, might this be yet another characteristic of the dejected lover, who frequently left tokens of his love at the door that was closed to him? Flowers were placed near the door, wine was spilled out in front of it, and perfume was poured on the door itself. The lack of specificity here allows for any one of these interpretations. The myrrh could have come from the man, who was clearly anxious for an intimate encounter as his importunity suggests. It could have been carried by the woman, who was really eager for his company, as the following verses describe. Actually, the origin of the myrrh does not seem to be the point of the image, for it is not mentioned again in this poem. Most likely, it is the presence of myrrh and the sensuous connotation that it carries that are important here.

When at last the woman opens the door, the man is gone. Some commentators believe that this is an example of coquetry gone wrong. However, the poetic nature of the Song and the recurrence of the seek-and-find theme warrant a different interpretation. Love poetry depicts what love itself often experiences, that is, the ebb and flow of feelings generated by events surrounding a possible rendezvous. There is often excitement and great anticipation, yet there is also the possibility that the slightest detail can frustrate the lovers' plans. Lovers must allow themselves to be vulnerable if they are honestly to express the character and depth of their love for each other. However, emotions can be misread, intentions can be misunderstood, and their vulnerability can make the lovers overly sensitive. This poetry concretely depicts this dimension of love.

The disappointment of the woman is acute (v. 6). Her emotional reaction made her faint. The Hebrew states: "my soul went forth" (cf. Gn 35:18, where the death of Rachel is recounted). We today would say, "I nearly died." One detail of this description is puzzling, that is, the cause of her swoon. An obvious reading of the Hebrew would be "when he spoke." This reading would only make sense if this verse was placed earlier in the poem, for the man spoke earlier, but not here. There is a relatively rare verb form (2 Chr 22:10; Pss 18:48; 47:4) that provides a reading that would be more comprehensible in this context. A possible cognate of the Arabic meaning "turn back or away," it would suggest that she became faint when she realized that he had left.

Using a parallel construction, the woman describes her search for her lover outside her room and her failure to find him there. As with an earlier poem (3:1f), her predicament precipitates an excursion into the city, where she once again encounters the sentinels (cf. 3:3). In the earlier poem, she enlists their help, inquiring of them concerning the whereabouts of her lover. In that poem, there is neither response to her query nor reaction to her presence in the city, alone and at night. Here, she asks no question of them, but they react violently toward her.

While the text offers no explanation for their fury, some commentators believe that they mistook her for a prostitute and responded accordingly. The nature of the garment she was wearing may account for this. This particular covering is only mentioned in one other place in the Bible, and there Isaiah lists it as an example of the superfluous finery of the daughters of Zion, finery that will be stripped from them by an aggrieved God (Is 3:23). This is not just a night-covering that the woman in the Song threw on in haste. It bespeaks luxury and at night could signify intended seduction (cf. Prv 7:10-12). According to Assyrian law, prostitutes wore no veil, and those who arrested them had the right to take their clothing. These customs might explain what is otherwise a strange occurrence in this poem.

Undeterred by the sentinels' mistreatment of her, the woman persists in her search for her lover, turning yet again to the daughters of Jerusalem and beseeching them for help (cf. 2:7; 3:5; 8:4). In other poems, the adjuration that she addresses to them is an oath, wherein she implores that they not disturb love. Here it is a simple request that they intervene to speak on her behalf should they come across her lover. This is the second time that the woman exclaims that she is "faint with love" (2:5). In the earlier passage her passion was the consequence of the pleasure she enjoyed in his embrace. Here it springs from the anguished longing for his company. The first part of this unit ends on a note of unfulfilled desire.

The Song of the Soul: There is very little in this first segment that lends itself to the nature-sensitive dimension that influences a contemporary spirituality's. One metaphor capitalizes on the gentleness of the dove in characterizing the woman (5:2). A second example, the incident of the woman's hands dripping myrrh as she opened the door to her already departed lover (5:5), uses myrrh to emphasize sensuousness and extravagance. In both cases, the poet is dependent on something from material creation for imagery that can capture not only the actual features of the woman, but also the sentiments that originally inspired the images and that the poet hopes will be once again elicited by them.

The specific images themselves address two very fundamental realities: the quality of gentleness that exists in so much of the natural world; and the exotic character of what nature so prodigally produces and freely provides. The utilization of such imagery shows that the artistic soul of the poet, whether writer or reader, resonates with the resplendence of the world within which it lives and of which it is an integral part. There is a rudimentary commonality that binds all of the natural world together, and poetic conceptualization is evidence of this.

Much more prominent here is the sexual dimension of contemporary spirituality that resonates with the erotic character of the poetry. The movement within the monologues and dialogues which comprise this part of the unit depicts the absence-presence-absence motif, and the sentiments expressed correspond to this movement. In the first place, the longing on the part of both of the lovers is intense. The man beseeches the woman to open to him. The names that he calls her ("my sister," "my beloved," "my dove," "my perfect one") make clear that, despite the reasons he gives while requesting entrance, his interest is more than shelter from the night elements. Though he leaves her door, he does not cease his desire for her. Instead he goes where he will ultimately be joined with her (in the garden).

Many of us have conflicting reactions to strong sexual passion. On the one hand, we long for it, we cherish it, we even sacramentalize it in marriage. On the other hand, we seem to be afraid of it, we caution against it, we sometimes even condemn it. Strong sexual passion is not something that human beings have devised; it was not our idea. Rather, it is part of our very nature as human beings. We grow into it as naturally as we gain stature and develop muscle.

Sexual passion is a unique kind of love, a love that has both a physical and a spiritual dimension to it. One side is no more superior to the other than Spring is to Fall. Since we are natural beings, everything about us has a physical dimension. Furthermore, genuine love has a transcendent aspect to it. They are both essential for life; they complement each other. As with all of the other wonders of the universe, they come from the hand of a loving and resourceful Creator.

94

The woman, on her part, overwhelmed by her own yearning, places herself in great jeopardy when she feels compelled to leave the security of her room and to venture out into the city. The fact that she had done this before without incident would be no guarantee that she would return unscathed a second time. Unconventional behavior, and her behavior certainly fit into that category, always carries risk. However, this danger did not deter her from her purpose. Her desire was stronger than any concern for safety. Love frequently constrains the lovers to forgo personal pursuits in the interest of the other. From the outside, such behavior may appear to be foolish, but love provides an entirely different perspective. Genuine devotion to the other is the only avenue open to true lovers.

The kind of longing depicted here springs from the desire for union with another, not merely from a selfish seeking for personal satisfaction. The expression found at the end of this unit, "I am my beloved's and my beloved is mine," makes this clear. In order to achieve such union, each lover would have to give generously to the other, while at the same time gratefully receive whatever the other was able and willing to offer. Such giving and receiving are only within the competence of an individual who is or is becoming self-possessed enough to be both unselfish and vulnerable. Genuine honesty and trusting surrender are also required, for such giving and receiving are based on an admission of one's inherent human incompleteness. Finally, this mutual exchange occurs on the deepest and most intimate level, the very sanctuary of the soul. Passionate longing and the pursuit of fulfillment that it engenders call for the best and most demanding of human virtues.

The double entendres in this poetry, used in reference to the behavior of both the woman and the man (vv. 2-6), reveal an eroticism that is undeniable but not explicit. The interplay of advance and retreat represents the tension between individual assertiveness and a self-control motivated by respect for the other, a tension that appears to have been kept in delicate balance here. All of this suggests an attitude toward sexuality that is neither inhibited not unrestrained, but one that is balanced and capable of enriching both lover and beloved. This is a sexuality that is both personally maturing and nurturing of others. It is a sexuality that is an authentic expression of self and an invitation for reciprocal self-expression in response.

Finally, there is much here that corresponds to contemporary spirituality. First, the woman is once again shown to be self-possessed and self-determined. She is able freely to offer herself, and she does this to the man whom she herself has chosen rather than to one chosen for her. She enjoys freedom of movement, which allows her to go unattended into the unfriendly city, where she endures violence and humiliation. She speaks assertively to the daughters of Jerusalem, unafraid to reveal the depth of her emotional state. Such self-assurance requires both a healthy self-image and great courage. All of these attitudes are highly prized today.

A second characteristic of this woman is her unabashed acknowledgement of her passionate reaction to her lover. This is a woman who is neither afraid of nor ashamed of strong emotion or of its physical manifestation. She is not a victim of some sexual stereotype that claims that women do not experience erotic sensations, or if they do, they do not enjoy them. Nor is she inhibited by a moral code that assigns blame to those who either enjoy such passion or who go in search of it. Throughout the poems, the couple's mutual sexual attraction appears to be quite natural, and so is the woman's response to it.

The final characteristic is the mutual nature of the love that is shared and outwardly displayed. Though told from the woman's point of view, the story makes it clear that neither partner is, on the one hand, inordinately aggressive nor, on the other, unduly withdrawn. At one time, it is the amorous longing of the man that directs the movement; at another, it is the equally forceful desire of the woman. The chauvinistic stereotypes of the assertive man and the passive woman are shattered here. Though not explicitly articulated, an anthropological presupposition operative in these poems accepts each person as a unique individual with distinctive attributes, interests, and capabilities. It is precisely this uniqueness that makes human love the exhilarating adventure that is portrayed here.

The Man of Her Dreams (5:9-6:3)

D   9How does your lover differ from any other,
    O most beautiful among women?
    How does your lover differ from any other,
      that you adjure us so?

B   10My lover is radiant and ruddy;
      he stands out among thousands.
   11His head is pure gold;
      his locks are palm fronds,
      black as the raven.
   12His eyes are like doves
      beside running waters,
   His teeth would seem bathed in milk,
      and are set like jewels.
   13His cheeks are like beds of spice
      with ripening aromatic herbs.
   His lips are red blossoms;
      they drip choice myrrh.

   14His arms are rods of gold
      adorned with chrysolites.
   His body is a work of ivory
      covered with sapphires.
   15His legs are columns of marble
      resting on golden bases.
   His stature is like the trees on Lebanon,
      imposing as the cedars.
   16His mouth is sweetness itself;
      he is all delight.

97

Such is my lover, and such my friend,
   O daughters of Jerusalem.

D   ¹Where has your lover gone,
   O most beautiful among women?
Where has your lover gone
   that we may seek him with you?

B   ²My lover has come down to his garden,
   to the beds of spice,
To browse in the garden
   and to gather lilies.
³My lover belongs to me and I to him;
   he browses among the lilies.

The daughters of Jerusalem reply to the woman's adjuration with a question concerned less with identifying characteristics of her beloved than with his uniqueness (5:9). The form of the question is repetitive parallelism. Its content plays off of the names that the lovers have earlier used for each other. The man is referred to as her beloved (*dôd*), and the woman is addressed as "most beautiful among women," one of his own terms of endearment for her. Although this part is separate from the dreamlike poem that precedes it, the question with which it begins acts as a link between the two. The word "adjure" refers to the woman's previous entreaty, while the question itself prepares for the woman's paean of praise that follows.

The woman launches into a monologue, using the *wasf* form to describe the matchless splendor of her beloved. Although this is the same literary form that the man used in his description of her (4:1-5), there are some distinctive features here. First, in the earlier poem, the man spoke directly to her in first person language, but this poem is a third person figurative description. Second, the imagery used here is quite different. In addition to the references to animals and vegetation used by the man, the woman also appeals to various natural features of gems and precious metals (cf. Dn 2:31-33). It would seem that his imagination was captured by nature, while hers was inspired both by nature and by some familiar statues of gods. It is interesting to note that she uses the first kind of imagery to extol the beauty of his head and facial features and the second kind to exemplify the splendor of the rest of his body.

The characterization itself is compelling. In language that is both graphic and hyperbolic, the woman praises the color, the sweetness, the beauty, and the strength of the man's body, proceeding from his head to his legs. She begins with a general description of his appearance (v. 10). Although the expression "radiant and ruddy" most likely refers to his complexion (cf. 1 Sm 16:12; 17:42; cf. Lam 4:7), it can describe his entire appearance, for an individual's countenance is often taken synecdochially to represent the total person. The word for radiance is rare and is elsewhere used to speak of the heat shimmering above the land (Is 18:4; Jer 4:11). In this instance the reference may suggest that the man both emanates radiance from within and resembles a luminous statue that reflects the brilliance of external light. In any case, he is incomparable, distinguished above all others (cf. Ps 3:6).

The next three verses (vv. 11-13) acclaim various features of the man's head. First the head itself is finest gold, similar to that of the head of the statue that appeared in the dream of king Nebuchadnezzar (Dn 2:32). The combination of the two synonyms for gold used here is not found elsewhere in the Bible, but similar constructions are (cf. Dn 10:5; 1 Kgs 10:18). This characterization yields several different possible meanings, none of which conflicts, but all of which contribute to a rich understanding of the image. On the most basic level, gold may refer to the color of the man's skin, a tone that suggests health and beauty. In addition, the resplendence of gold suggests the magnitude of the man's worth. Finally, since this precious metal was used in the construction of images of royalty and gods, this metaphor may be yet another comparison of the man with such statuary.

It is difficult to decide the exact characterization intended for his hair (cf. 5:2). The word used to describe it appears no place else in the Bible. It has been rendered both palm fronds and hillock. While the specific reference is unclear, the point of the image is the same in either case. The man's hair is thick and wavy like palm branches or like rolling hills. Compared to the blackness of the raven, this hair must have been an astonishing sight against the golden skin of the man. It is no wonder that the woman asserts that he is radiant (v. 10).

In two earlier poems, the man declares that the woman's eyes are doves (1:15; 4:1). That identification included no elaboration. Here it is the woman who compares the man's eyes with doves (v. 12). However, the description that follows this comparison is not of the eyes, but of the doves. They are standing by springs of water (cf. Jl 3:18 [Heb]), bathed in milk (cf. Jb 29:6), and firmly set. (The meaning of the Hebrew is uncertain, leading some to suggest that "bathed in milk" and "firmly set" refer to the man's teeth. Such a reading would correspond to the man's earlier description of the woman in 4:1f.)

This last characterization highlights the abundance of water. When applied to the man, the images suggest that there is a liquid quality to his eyes. There is a pun here that is lost in translation. The same Hebrew word means both eyes and spring. The man's eyes also resemble the smooth thickness of milk and the calm behavior of the doves; they are soft and they are gentle. The contrast of color in these last two metaphors is striking. The hair is black as a raven; the eyes are white as a dove. The visual imagery paints a compelling portrait of a man who mesmerizes this woman.

The *wasf* continues its praise of the exceptional beauty of the man, appealing to the intoxicating properties of certain fragrances. As was the case with the visual metaphors, the comparisons here are hyperbolic overstatements and should

100

not be forced into literal interpretations, since lovers frequently speak in superlatives. The first reference is to cheeks, not whiskers as some commentators argue. Previously the man had marvelled at the beauty of the ornamentation of the woman's cheeks (1:10), now she marvels at the exhilarating scent of his.

The Hebrew word translated as "bed" in this verse has puzzled many commentators. It can also be translated as "towers" and be a reference to cones placed on the top of a man's head, the fragrant ointment within them dripping down his head and neck. This interpretation of the ambiguous reference is probably why some commentators read cheeks as whiskers (cf. Ps 113:2, the beard of Aaron). Others follow the Septuagint reading, change the vocalization of the Hebrew, and produce some form of the verb "to put forth" or "to grow." This particular reading would not necessitate understanding cheeks as whiskers.

All of this notwithstanding, the Hebrew can be read as "cheeks" and "tower," and there is no need to change the reading in either case. There are four other references to tower in the Song. In each instance it characterizes a part of the woman's body: her neck (4:4; 7:4), her nose (7:4), and her breasts (8:10). The poetic exaggeration in each case is obvious. None of these allusions is intended to be taken literally. Instead, there is some characteristic of the tower that is applied to the respective body-part. Tower should be understood in the same way in this case. The tenor of the metaphor may be the capacity of the tower to contain an abundance of precious perfumes, thus overflowing with exotic fragrance. This is another example of the hyperbole for which the *wasf* is famous.

Having compared the man's eyes with doves, the woman uses another image that was previously applied to her: His lips are lilies (cf. 2:1f). Although the image is the same in both instances, the tenor of its comparison is quite different. The woman was compared to its beauty and delicacy. The point of the image here is the nectar emitted by the flower. In an earlier poem the woman's lips were described as dripping honey (4:11), suggesting that her mouth is overflowing with delectability. That image was interpreted in a twofold manner, as a metaphor for her enticing speech and as a description of passionate kissing. In this poem, the man's lips drip myrrh, a resin with intoxicating qualities that always take on an erotic meaning in the Song (1:13; 3:6; 4:6, 14; 5:1, 5). Most likely, the allusion in this verse is to the man's passionate kisses.

The next two verses are replete with images that suggest statuary. The first metaphor is somewhat ambiguous (v. 14). The Hebrew word is really "hand." However, the description that follows, rods of gold filled with jewels, does not fit this meaning well, unless the reference is to fingers or arms. If this is the case, this image would yield a picture of a bronzed man bedecked with jeweled rings or armlets. There is ample evidence that ancient representations of gods were so fashioned. The grandeur of such statues and the value of the metals used in their construction and ornamentation made them apt subjects for comparison.

Moving further down his body, the woman praises the man's belly, clearly a provocative allusion. The generous use of double entendre throughout the poems leaves this particular reference open to interpretation. This detail is reminiscent of the statue in Nebuchadnezzar's dream (Dn 2:32). In this paean, the belly is said to be like smooth ivory covered with sapphires or lapis lazuli. Blue stones against an ivory background create a curious picture if the intent is a literal description of the man's trunk.

As with the other metaphors that include precious metals or jewels in their comparison, the reference here is to some characteristic other than its actual appearance. It may be that the contrast between the ivory and the sapphire is meant to highlight the resplendence of the gem, which, in several places in the Bible, is associated with the deity (cf. Ex 24:10, where sapphire is used in the pavement beneath God's feet; Ez 1:26, where it is the composition of the divine throne itself). Some form of divine statuary may have inspired this exaltation of the man's torso.

Praise of the man's body ends with a characterization of his legs and feet as marble columns set on bases of gold (v. 15; cf. Eccl 26:18 for a similar description of the legs and feet of a good wife). The strength of marble and the costliness of gold complete this picture of extraordinary worth. His head is gold, as are his feet. From head to toe, the man is priceless. There is no base element in this image, no clay feet (cf. Dn 2:33f). The man is the embodiment of elegance, statue and quality. The majesty of this man, tall and strong, beautiful and sweet smelling, is compared to the magnificent cedars of Lebanon. The *wasf* is complete.

The woman concludes her description of the man with a comment about his palate. She states that it is sweet wine (cf. Neh 8:10 for the same translation of the word). Since in several other places in the Song this reference is to the sweetness of kisses (cf. 1:2; 2:4; 7:10), it would seem appropriate to read this verse in that way as well. This is not to say that there is no allusion here to loving speech. Instead, this passage should be interpreted in a way similar to the reading of an earlier one, where the man extols the woman's mouth for both its enticing speech and its passionate kisses (4:11).

The reply to the daughters of Jerusalem closes with the woman emphatically stating: "Such is my lover, and such my friend." The double declaration corresponds to the double question originally posed by the daughters (5:9). They had questioned her as to the preeminence of her beloved. She has now described him in a way that cannot be matched, much less exceeded.

The second set of questions posed, presumably by the daughters of Jerusalem, deals with the whereabouts of this remarkable man. The form of these questions is similar to the earlier set (5:9): a question; an epithet; repetition of the question (this time with a slight variation); a dependent clause. The first set of questions is merely an inquiry; what makes this man extraordinary? This second set seeks information that will enable the daughters to accompany the woman in her search for her beloved (*dôd*). The woman is referred to once again as "most beautiful among women" (cf. 5:9), a term of endearment used of her by the man (cf. 1:8). The pet name ascribed to him (*dôd*) is used five times in these three verses.

The woman's answer suggests that she knew where the man could be found. This seems to conflict with her earlier outcry upon opening her door and finding him gone: "I sought him but I did not find him; I called to him but he did not answer" (5:6). This apparent disparity can be explained if we remember that the Song probably originated as a collection of various similar but unrelated poems. In its final form, the disparity furthers the absence-presence-absence character of the work.

The woman states that the man has gone down to his garden (v. 2). In an earlier poem, the garden was a metaphor for the woman (4:12-16). After she gives him access to the garden (4:16), it is referred to as "his garden" (4:16–5:1). The phrase "bed of spices," though identical to the reference to the man's cheeks (5:13), is most likely an allusion to the delectable nature of the woman, whose charms are compared to exotic spices (4:10, 14; 5:1). Just as she is the garden, so she is the bed of spices to which he goes down. The man has gone to enjoy the pleasures of the woman.

There in the garden(s) the man pastures his flock and gathers lilies (a variation of 2:16, where he pastures the flocks among the lilies). Since both garden and lilies have referred to the charms of the woman, and pasturing his flocks has referred to lovemaking (cf. 2:16), the woman is alluding to an anticipated intimate interlude. This is confirmed by a declaration of mutual possession (v. 3; cf. 2:16 for the

104

expression in reverse order). She is his: "my beloved" (1:9, 15: 2:2, 10, 13); "my beautiful one" (2:13); "my dove" (2:14), and he is hers: "my lover" (1:13, 14, 16; 2:3, 8, 9, 10). This simple yet passionate expression captures the essence of the entire Song. It describes total reciprocal self-giving and acceptance.

The Song of the Soul: This final part of the unit contains material that resonates with strong contemporary themes. First and most obviously, the woman very graphically and in great detail extols features of the man's body. This is a reverse of the customary practice of men commenting on women's physical qualities. It belies the misconception that women are not at all interested in the male physique, but are only concerned about how men will care for them and provide for their every need. The woman has not only taken notice of his appearance, but has thought long and hard about what she has seen, for she is able to describe his features in imagery that is well crafted.

Secondly, while she artfully describes the properties of his head and face, properties that can easily be observed without risking being accused of indecorous scrutiny, she directs her attention to his belly, legs and feet as well. The woman has a robust appreciation for his entire body, and she celebrates it with unabashed candor. This is not some prurient fascination; it is genuine admiration of the form and substance of the man she loves. This preoccupation may appear unusual, since it is presumed that women are not accustomed to fix their attention on the bodily attributes of men. The one exception to this is women's appreciation of men's muscular distinction, which was seen as a source of protection. However, the human body, whether female or male, is an incomparable work of art, and no praise of it will ever adequately do homage to the creativity of the Artist who produced it.

A second and related dimension of this spirituality is the

woman's straightforward attitude toward sexuality. Her descriptions of the charms of her lover are both arrestingly poetic and discreetly provocative. She uses imagery that is sensuous but not obscene; her references are earthy but not vulgar; her adulation is explicit but not lewd. It is clear that for her sexuality is an integral component of her world and of her love, not an artifice with which to manipulate or a weapon to be used against another. It is strange that anyone would think that women have little or no interest in sexual passion. Their dissatisfaction with lovemaking that is rushed, their yearning for romance and the signs of affection that accompany it, are indications of a vigorous sexual appetite. A woman's interest may be different from a man's, but she is interested nonetheless. As a God-given desire it should not be disdained.

This part of the unit ends on a note that is of greatest importance today, that is, mutuality. After the woman sings the praises of the man, she exclaims that she is his and he is hers. Mutuality is not the same as equality. The former is a dynamic concept, which includes the notion of exchange or balance. The latter, which suggests sameness, is more a condition of static being. Mutuality respects difference, realizing that the give and take within relationships can be reciprocal without being strictly equal. Partners do not give exactly the same thing to each other, but they must be mutually respectful, attentive, and engaged. This is the kind of relationship that is expected and demanded today, a relationship built on reverence of the fundamental human dignity of the other.

Finally, the metaphors used by the woman in her celebration of the marvels of the man she loves are all nature-sensitive, fashioned out of the very stuff of the earth. She is dependent for her poetry on the vivid colors and exotic scents of animals and plants, and on the brilliance of gems and precious ores. Captivated by the natural comeliness of her lover, she compares him to the majesty of other treasures of nature. In this metaphorical exchange, the characteristics of one become the characteristics of the other. Thus, the exaltation of the man also gives honor to the element of nature to which he is compared.

VI

Admiration and Desire

The limits of the fifth unit (6:4–8:4) are determined by two distinct refrains: "My lover belongs to me and I to him" (6:3) and "I adjure you, daughters of Jerusalem" (8:4). The unit itself is a composite made up of a *wasf* and a song of admiration proclaimed by the man (6:4-7; 8-10), a short statement by the woman (vv. 11-12), an address to the woman by unknown speakers and her brief response (7:1), a second *wasf* and poem of admiration by the man (vv. 2-6; 7-10), and two love monologues by the woman (vv. 11-14; 8:1-4). The first *wasf* and poem by the man comprise a section themselves, set off by the *inclusio* "as awe-inspiring as bannered troops" (vv. 4, 10). The similarities between this unit and an earlier one (3:6–5:1) are striking; some of the imagery is identical.

A Vision of Loveliness Revisited (6:4-7)

G   ⁴You are as beautiful as Tirzah, my beloved,
  as lovely as Jerusalem,
  as awe-inspiring as bannered troops.
 ⁵Turn your eyes from me,
  for they torment me.
 Your hair is like a flock of goats
  streaming down from Gilead.
  ⁶Your teeth are like a flock of ewes
  which come up from the washing,

108

All of them big with twins,
　none of them thin and barren.
⁷Your cheek is like a half-pomegranate
　behind your veil.

With minor variations, the first *wasf* (6:4-7) is a shortened form of one found earlier (cf. 4:1-7). They both begin with a declaration of the woman's beauty (cf. 1:15; 4:1, 7), which is followed by a detailed description of her captivating physical features. Her beauty is compared here to the splendors of two prominent cities. While the custom of portraying cities as female is routine, conversely, characterizing a woman as a city is less common. This woman is compared to Tirzah, the capital of the northern kingdom of Israel dating from the reign of Jeroboam to that of Omri, and to Jerusalem, the capital of Judah. Like these proud cities, she possesses regal demeanor and extravagant splendor. Comparing her to a walled city serves as yet another symbol of the enclosed and guarded nature of her person (see garden and fountain, 4:12).

The Hebrew text mentions awe-inspiring banners but not an army, as many translations render the passage. However, the use of a form of the same adjective in another place in the Bible suggests a military image (cf. Hb 1:7), hence many translators include it here. While using such imagery to describe a woman may seem strange to the contemporary reader, it does fit with references found earlier in the Song, namely, the tower of David with its battle accouterments (4:4) and the fortified cities mentioned above. The point of the comparison is the appeal of the woman's physical features. She is beautiful, comely and awe-inspiring. In order to concretize his praise, the man simply chose three outstanding realities from his experience, realities which are renowned for their commanding splendor.

The order of the *wasf* that follows (vv. 5-7) is the same as that found in the earlier parallel *wasf* (4:1-3). The man's attention is drawn first to the woman's eyes and then to her hair, her teeth and her cheeks (reference to the lips is omitted here). Mention of the powerful cities and the spectacular banners (v. 4) sets the context for understanding the *wasf*. In this poem, the delicate nature scene found elsewhere gives way to allusions to magnificence and strength.

There seems to be a gradual intensification in the power that the woman's eyes exert over the man. First they are calming, reminding him of the gentleness of the doves (4:1). Then they ravish his heart (4:9). Here they are so overwhelming that he pleads with her to divert her gaze (6:5). This description of her eyes is consistent with his allusion to her awe-inspiring character (v.4). While it may seem incongruous to some, the connection between beauty and terror is well attested in romantic literature.

With the exception of a few slight emendations, the language in this *wasf* is identical to that found in the earlier one. The woman's flowing black hair is compared to a flock of goats moving down the slopes of Gilead (the word "Mount" is omitted here); her white teeth are like paired ewes ("shorn" is omitted); her cheeks are flush like a pomegranate. No satisfactory explanation has been given for this repetition other than the fact that recurrence of themes and phrases is a characteristic of poetry.

Singular Beauty (6:8-10)

[8] There are sixty queens, eighty concubines,
   and maidens without number—
[9] One alone is my dove, my perfect one,
   her mother's chosen,
   the dear one of her parent.
The daughters saw her and declared her fortunate,
   the queens and concubines, and they sang her praises;

D   ¹⁰Who is this that comes forth like the dawn,
      as beautiful as the moon, as resplendent as the sun,
      as awe-inspiring as bannered troops?

After the man praises the woman directly, he then speaks about her in the third person. The poem in which he does this (vv. 8-10) is more than a song of admiration. It is a kind of boasting song, a declaration of the singularity of the woman. In it, image upon image proclaims her distinctiveness. Elements of this poem also resemble the earlier *wasf*. Both contain the same question: "Who is this?" (3:6; 6:10). The first *wasf* is preceded by the description of a royal procession (3:6-10); here the mention of royalty instead follows the *wasf* (6:8-9). The earlier poem speaks of sixty mighty men (3:7); this one speaks of sixty royal women (6:8-9). Mothers are prominent in both poems; Solomon is crowned by his mother (3:11), and the beloved woman of the poem is favored by hers (6:9).

The numerical sequence, sixty-eighty-innumerable, a Semitic way of designating a large and indefinite number, underscores the woman's uniqueness. The three categories that comprise the sequence designate various social classes: queens, secondary wives, and maidens. In this literary form, as the numbers increase, the social status decreases. The expression need not allude to any particular royal household, as some commentators suggest. It certainly does not reflect an Israelite royal harem, since the Bible uses the designation "king's wife" not the title "queen" when referring to a royal wife. This sequence may merely be a ranking of women, whose social and collective attributes are compared to the charms of the woman of the Song, and are found wanting. It continues the royal fiction found in several other places in the Song (1:12; 3:6-11).

In contrast to any display of royal splendor, this woman stands out as one of a kind (v. 9). In a threefold construction,

111

the man praises her distinctiveness. The first two phrases are introduced by the same expression: "One alone" to this man, who calls her "my dove, my perfect one" (cf. 5:2); "one alone" to her own mother. The second and third phrases form a parallelism: "One alone" to her own mother; "the dear one of her parent." The phrase that characterizes her uniqueness in relation to her mother should not be understood as an identification of her as an only child. Rather, it denotes the singular affection that her mother has toward her. In other words, even within her own family she is in a class by herself.

Three groups of women, namely queens, secondary wives and daughters (a synonym for maidens? cf. v. 8), join the man in exalting the woman he loves. The daughters saw her and called her happy, using the word that introduces the literary form known as beatitude (happy are . . .), while the queens and secondary wives praised her. The very women who under other circumstances would be the ones receiving the praise are here showering it upon her. All of this shows that the man's declaration of his love's incomparability is not merely the exaggeration that frequently accompanies passion. Instead, it is an appraisal that is shared by those within her own household, as well as by those who may not know her, but who have seen her.

The exclamatory question "Who is this . . . ?" (v. 10) is a rhetorical form intended to draw public notice to the object of attention (cf. 3:6; 8:5). The Hebrew verb suggests that the woman enjoys a view from above, looking down upon the others. This can refer to an actual position of height or to one of status. The latter understanding better fits the reference here, for the incomparability of the woman's beauty as described above situates her in a position of superiority in relation to others. This superiority is explicated in the characterization that follows.

The woman is compared to the breaking dawn, to the white moon and the hot sun, and to awe-inspiring banners (of an army?). Although the character of the Song dictates

112

that these references be understood as comparisons with natural phenomena, the mythological allusions behind the comparisons are quite clear. The goddess of the dawn played an important role in Canaanite mythology, as did the sun and the moon. The influence of such deities can be seen in the Israelite prohibition against the worship of them (cf. Dt 17:3; Jer 8:2). The phrasing of these prohibitions throws light on the meaning of the awe-inspiring banners mentioned here. Once again, the context suggests a military allusion. Just as the earlier juxtaposition of the phrase with references to Tirzah and Jerusalem suggested the military banners of a fortified city (v. 4), so here its conjunction with the heavenly phenomena suggests a cosmic army.

The beauty of this woman is incredible. In an attempt to describe it, the man utilizes whatever comparison is within his reach. He likens her to the splendor of two of Israel's most celebrated cities, to the breathtaking beauty of the natural world around him, to the grandeur associated with royalty, and to the unparalleled magnificence of the cosmos. As descriptive and as extravagant as these comparisons may be, they do not seem able to capture the essence of this woman's comeliness as perceived by the man who loves her. All he can do is offer an inadequate sketch of the resplendence that has left him spellbound.

The Song of the Soul: This description of the woman contains several features found in a contemporary spirituality. Its nature-sensitive character can be seen in several ways. First, the comparisons with characteristics of the goats, the ewes and the pomegranates demonstrate an appreciation for the sights that their movements create and the colors that their appearances display. Had not the poet an eye for and an appreciation of the beauty that is intrinsic to the natural world, elements of this world would not have been used as metaphors to represent the natural beauty of the woman.

113

The significance of natural elements is also seen in the magnificence that is produced when human beings rework these elements and fashion them into various artifacts. If a city is truly splendid, it is only because the artistry of the builders of that city is able to bring out the splendor of the material of which it is made. Although at times it can ruthlessly exploit, human manufacture does not always or necessarily violate the integrity of natural elements. On the contrary, genuine artistry can add a dimension of beauty to raw material. Therefore, while praise of a city is indeed recognition of human ingenuity, it is also celebration of the merit of the materials used in the building.

There is a very close bond between religious imagination and artistic creativity. They both spring from an intangible insight that looks at life and at the world in innovative ways. It is difficult to envision religious imagination devoid of an artistic element, and many believe that artistic originality transcends the banal much like religious inspiration does. However we understand these abilities, they both see beneath the surface of reality and there discover a dimension that can only be called spiritual.

Finally, the artistic eye of the poet moves beyond the immediate world of nature to the broader world of the cosmos. Heavenly bodies are characterized as fair-white (the moon), bright-hot (the sun), and awe-inspiring (the banners), descriptive words that demonstrate the poet's perception of these cosmic realities. There is not the familiarity here that is obvious in the descriptions of the goats, the ewes and the pomegranates. There is, instead, the kind of reverence that one experiences in the presence of an exceptional force or reality. These cosmic references lay bare the poet's nature-sensitive recognition of the grandeur of the universe and the subordinate role that humankind plays in its operations. The magnificence of the universe is the background for the references to the beauty of the woman. Allusions to nature's splendor highlight her superiority in comparison with others.

There is a strong quality to these references to the woman. Drawn from three quite different settings—urban, rural and cosmic—very powerful imagery is used in each case in comparing the woman's appearance. The cities may be beautiful and comely, but they are also awe-inspiring. The animals and fruit may be pleasing to the sight, but they are also robust. The cosmic referents are clearly daunting. The beauty described here does not conform to any feminine stereotype of carefully crafted, soft, fragile loveliness. It is an open beauty, not protected or hidden from view. It is an honest beauty, neither seductive nor in any other way manipulative. It is an unpretentious beauty, authentic and straightforward.

The extraordinariness of these images is found in their authenticity. There is no need for them to conform to the artificial standards of some outside force. They are what they are, and there is exceptional charm in that. This is the kind of standard by which beauty is judged today. It is a standard that is determined by the intrinsic nature of something, not by its value in relation to something else. More and more people today insist that human beings are beautiful in themselves, with all of their individuality and uniqueness. We are realizing that people should not be compelled to conform to a standard of size, shape, coloring or age determined by the arbitrary tastes of some select group. While the imagery in this poetry may strike the present-day reader as strange, the qualities that it depicts are quite contemporary.

The Nut Garden (6:11-12)

B   [11]I came down to the nut garden
      to look at the fresh growth of the valley,
   To see if the vines were in bloom,
      if the pomegranates had blossomed.
   [12]Before I knew it, my heart had made me
      the blessed one of my kinswomen.

This short passage (6:11-12) is very difficult to translate and to interpret. The identity of the speaker is a disputed point. Some claim that it is the man, since throughout the earlier poems the woman is characterized as a garden (4:12,16) to which the man goes (4:16; 5:1; 6:2). However, in an upcoming poem (7:11-14), it is the woman, using the same uncommon language as is found here ("blossomed" and "in bloom," 6:11; 7:13), who invites the man into the fields to see the blossoming of spring. This has led other commentators to maintain that it is the woman speaking here as well.

Although the word for nut appears no place else in the Bible, its frequent use in later Rabbinic literature helps us to identify it as a walnut. According to Near Eastern mythology, the nut was thought to possess both magical and sexual properties, just as vines and pomegranates do in the Song. Thus, whatever the exact meaning of this reference may be, its erotic character is unmistakable.

The next verse (v. 12), considered the most difficult in the entire Song, offers no help in identifying the speaker. As it stands, the Hebrew is unintelligible. Most interpreters emend the text, thereby determining its meaning rather than discovering it. The gender designation given to the previous verse is usually attributed to this one as well. Either the woman speaks both verses (the position held here), or the man does. The verse itself begins with an expression that describes the speaker as being taken by surprise. Before she knew it, the woman was transported to the chariot of a nobleman. This image corresponds to an earlier one, where reference to the litter of Solomon contributes to the royal fiction employed in the Song. Both the litter and the chariot are majestic vehicles of transportation, vehicles which provide ample opportunity for the passengers to engage in amorous behavior.

Despite the brevity of this passage, it creates a scene that corresponds perfectly to both the nature-sensitive and the erotic character of the Song and to the kind of spirituality

116

that it supports. As was the case in a previous poem (2:11-13), the freshness of springtime becomes a metaphor for representing the youthfulness and the untouched innocence of the relationship between the woman and the man. This youthfulness and innocence should not be confused with naiveté. The poems depict the awakening of spring and new love, not of pubescence. The youthfulness and innocence are marks of the healthy, straightforward forces of energy and attraction present in all living things. Nature is never ashamed to disclose its life-force or the fruits of its life-giving properties. Neither is genuine love.

The erotic character of the poem is seen again in the connotations associated with the nut garden. The woman went to a garden where the fruit had the properties of an aphrodisiac. She exhibits no shame, nor does the poet criticize her for such behavior. Pursuing sexual delights is neither denounced nor perceived as extraordinary. It is as natural as is the onset of spring or the ripening of autumn. Sexuality is an intrinsic dimension of what it means to be a natural, human creature in a world of other natural creatures. It influences many of our preferences and it motivates much of our activity. It is an integral facet of our spirituality.

Finally, this short passage once again depicts the woman in a manner compatible with a contemporary view. She is self-motivated, neither obsessed with nor intimidated by her own sexual interests. It is the man she loves who is the object of her pursuit, not sexual satisfaction in itself. According to current standards, this is a very healthy woman.

The Dance (7:1-6)

D   ¹Turn, turn, O Shulammite,
    turn, turn, that we may look at you!

B   Why would you look at the Shulammite
    as at the dance of the two companies?

D   ²How beautiful are your feet in sandals,
       O prince's daughter!
    Your rounded thighs are like jewels,
       the handiwork of an artist.
    ³Your navel is a round bowl
       that should never lack for mixed wine.
    Your body is a heap of wheat
       encircled with lilies.
    ⁴Your breasts are like twin fawns,
       the young of a gazelle.
    ⁵Your neck is like a tower of ivory.
    Your eyes are like the pools in Heshbon
       by the gate of Bath-rabbim.
    Your nose is like the tower on Lebanon
       that looks toward Damascus.
    ⁶Your head rises like Carmel;
       your hair is like draperies of purple;
       a king is held captive in its tresses.

The introductory verse of the *wasf* (7:1[Heb]) yields several
interpretations, all of which depend upon how the preceding
passage was understood. The first word can be translated
"turn" or "return." If it is the woman who went down to the
nut garden in the previous passage (6:11), she could be called
upon here to "return." Furthermore, if she has been taken by
surprise and has been transported by fancy to some kind of
chariot (v. 12), she could be called to return to her senses.
However, the theme of dance, which follows this vocative
expression (7:1b) and the rhythmic impression produced by
the fourfold repetition of the word itself suggest that it
should be translated "turn." Since the Hebrew verb allows
both meanings, the problem is more in the translation, which
requires the choice of only one rendering.

The identity of the Shulammite has also perplexed interpreters. Is the designation an allusion to Shunem, the
Jezreelite village from which came Abishag, the Davidic wife,
whose possible future with Adonijah threatened the sover-
eignty of Solomon (1 Kgs 2:13-25)? This view would give

historical mooring to the Song. Is the word a form of Shulmnîtu, the name of a Mesopotamian goddess of war? This view would support the military imagery that some translations favor. Or is the term merely a derivation of *šlm*, the Hebrew basis for the words Solomon, Jerusalem and peace (*shalom*)? This latter explanation appears to be the most likely. In support of this view, the character of the Song with its Solomonic fiction, its frequent references to Jerusalem, and its description of idyllic settings invites an understanding of the word that includes all three of the semantic referents of the third possible interpretation.

The request of the bystanders to "turn" is answered by the woman's inquiry: "Why do you want to look upon me?" This cannot be the response of a naive maiden who is unaware of her beauty, for the woman herself attested to it earlier (1:5). The meaning of this phrase hinges on the way the rest of the verse is understood. To what kind of dance does the text refer? The Hebrew word is in dual form, indicating a double of attendants. A double group of what? armies? dancers? spectators? The Hebrew is not clear.

Is this a dance of victory after war? If so, how does this theme of conflict and violence fit into the context of love poetry? Is it a sword dance, a part of ancient Near Eastern wedding celebration? This can hardly be the meaning, since nowhere in the Song is the couple said to be married. Does the woman's demure response originate from a sense of propriety that would allow her to expose herself to her lover but not to the general public? It might be that the bystanders urge the woman to dance so that they can observe her beauty, but she resists, insisting that she is not some common camp dancer. She might consider performing an erotic dance for the man alone, but she is not an exhibitionist.

The *wasf* itself (7:2-6) is similar to the two earlier ones (4:1-7; 5:10-16) in that it describes various parts of the body in an orderly sequence. However, whereas the order of the other poems was downward, this poem begins its description with the feet and moves upward to the head. The reason for this change in direction may be that the man's attention was first caught by the woman's dancing feet. From there, his gaze moves up her body. Some of the comparisons are similes, using the comparative particle "like." Others are metaphors that, for the sake of forceful description, apply to an object a characteristic that does not literally belong to it.

The man begins his song of praise with an exclamation of the beauty of the woman (cf. 4:1; 6:4; 7:7). Here, it is specifically the beauty of her sandaled feet, a point not to be too quickly overlooked. Since rural women and professional dancers normally went barefoot, sandals were considered a decorative addition, more easily available to women of noble or upper-class status (cf. Ez 16:10; Jdt 10:4; 16:9). While this feature, along with the designation of her as a noble woman, may further the royal fiction, the sandals also play a significant role in the idea of the dance. The word used for feet is better translated "footstep." This implies movement, rhythm, even sound. In fact, this is the only word that suggests that the woman is in fact dancing. If she were barefoot, the steps of her feet could certainly be seen. However, with sandals the rhythm of her footsteps can also be heard.

The form of most of the comparisons in this *wasf* is consistent. A part of the body is named, and comparison with something else is made. Parallel construction then extends the description of some feature of one of the elements of the metaphor. This feature should not be applied to the female body part. In other words, the jewelry, not the woman's thighs, is the handiwork of the artisan; the bowl, not her navel, never lacks mixed wine; the wheat, not the woman's belly, is encircled with lilies; the fawns, not her breasts, are the twins of the gazelle.

The description of the woman's thighs (v. 2) contains four instances of words that appear in no other place in the Bible, resulting in an interpretation that can only be approximate.

First, the exact part of the body alluded to is not certain. The adjective ("turning") used in the description of this body part can refer to sinuous movement as well as to curvaceous shape. This has led to the identification of the upper thighs or even the buttocks, both of which are rounded and would shimmy if the hips were undulating in some kind of dance. This particular physical feature is likened to precious jewelry, the handiwork of an artisan. The reference may be to a type of ornamentation that women wore suspended around their hips, ornamentation that flowed and waved and, perhaps, shimmered with the swaying. This would certainly catch the fancy of those watching her movements.

The roundness of the woman's body continues to hold the attention of the man as his eyes move to her navel and her belly (v. 3). Because the description within the *wasf* is upward, and the navel is above not beneath the belly, which is also extolled later in this poem, some commentators maintain that the reference here is to the vulva. However, strict adherence to the structure of the body is not observed in other places in the poem (eyes are described before the nose), and so emendation for the sake of such ordering does not seem to be necessary here. The navel, pressed into the body, would have a concave shape, rounded like a vessel that held wine mixed with water or honey and spices. Since the umbilical cord was the original source of nourishment, the navel has always retained this connection with life and sensuality.

The man's admiring gaze next fixes itself on the woman's belly, which is compared to wheat. After wheat was cut, it was left piled in the fields. The image bespeaks roundness, softness and a tawny color, all allusions that fit well the character of the belly. In order that the piled wheat not be blown away or eaten by roaming animals, it was frequently protected by a hedge of thorns or thistles. This might explain the circle of lilies mentioned here. Since the context of the Song is idyllic, and the referent of the metaphor is the woman's belly, a circle of lilies seems more in keeping with the sense of the Song than would a hedge of thorns. Finally, since wheat is a staple of life, this particular metaphor also carries the notion of fecundity and sustenance. As the earlier characterization of the navel suggested liquid nourishment, so this representation of the belly suggests solid food.

In the identical words found in an earlier *wasf* (v. 4; cf. 4:5), the woman's breasts are compared to fawn twins of the gazelle, an animal renowned for its grace and beauty and whose name comes from the Hebrew word meaning splendor or glory (cf. Is 4:2; 28:5). "Fawns" suggests a youthful body and all of the comeliness that accompanies it. The praise of the woman's breasts is probably directed toward their firmness and shapeliness, characteristics which by themselves can inspire admiration. Most likely, the metaphor functions here in the same way as it did in the earlier poem, with one slight variation. The color of the fawns is the same as the wheat in the previous metaphor.

A few points should be noted. In the first *wasf*, the fawns are said to feed among the lilies. It is probably omitted here because of the reference to lilies in the preceding metaphor. Furthermore, a second descriptive phrase would alter the literary construction that has been followed in the *wasf* to this point (specifically, mention of a body part, followed by a metaphor, ending with an added descriptive phrase). Finally, various conclusions have been drawn concerning the state of dress of the woman. The vividness of the descriptions imply that her body can be clearly seen. It is unlikely that she is naked, since that would be out of character of a woman of noble background. She may be wearing a diaphanous veil-like garment, which would allow the contours of her body to be seen through its cover. Though a covering, such a garment would be quite revealing and thus provocative.

The woman's neck is compared to a tower (v. 5). In an earlier *wasf*, it was likened to the tower of David with all of its military trappings (4:4). Here it is a tower of ivory. Most

122

likely, the point of the comparison is the value of the material and the stately elegance of the tower itself. In extolling the physical preeminence of the man she loves, the woman herself had likened his torso to ivory (5:14). Here he returns the compliment.

Though not actually constructed of ivory, several royal furnishings were inlaid with it. Kings were said to live in ivory houses (1 Kgs 22:39) or palaces (Ps 45:8) and sit on ivory thrones (2 Chr 9:17). In their attempt to emulate the royalty, the affluent slept on ivory beds (Am 6:4). The value of ivory is indisputable. The creamy color of ivory, suggestive of the color of the woman's skin, may also play a role in this comparison, just as the height of the tower denotes stateliness and pride.

This representation of the woman's neck is the only metaphor in the *wasf* that docs not correspond to the literary pattern described above. It does not include a descriptive phrase elaborating some feature of the tower. Some scholars believe that originally there was a parallel phrase that was lost or misplaced. The metaphor itself may have been added as an afterthought, for in the very same verse, the woman's nose is compared to a tower. It is unusual that a poem, otherwise so carefully crafted, would employ the same image for such different physical features.

Having characterized the woman's neck, the man goes on to describe the features of her face and head. Just as his eyes were associated with springs of water (5:12), so her eyes are called pools. Heshbon, an Amorite royal city, is east of Jerusalem in the modern country of Jordan. This is the third city mentioned in the description of the woman. Like Tirzah and Jerusalem (6:2), mention of this city resonates with the royal fiction seen so frequently in the Song. Recent excavations there have unearthed the remains of huge reservoirs of remarkable masonry, which probably held the water supply for this city renowned for its abundant fertility and rich vineyards. The metaphor suggests water that is tranquil, not flowing as spring water would be. It is deep water, mysterious. When applied to eyes, the image is quite sensuous.

The pools are located at the gate called "daughter of many." Just as cities were generally characterized as feminine, so the surrounding villages that were dependent upon these cities were referred to as daughters. The reservoirs, normally located near the gates, supplied water to city and villages alike. Therefore, the gate closest to the water supply would most likely be the busiest gate of the city, the "gate of the daughter of many."

The woman's nose is said to be like a tower of Lebanon, an image that strikes modern sensitivities as strange, even unflattering. However, each time the word tower has been used as a comparison of some physical feature of either the man or the woman, its primary focus has been something other than height. When the woman's neck was likened to the tower of David (4:4), the point of comparison was the adornment that it displayed. When it is likened to a tower of ivory (7:4), it is the stateliness that is suggested. Accordingly, the point of the present reference may be a feature other than height.

Mention of Lebanon conjures up another word, frankincense. These two words are clearly associated in several places in the Song (4:11, 6-8). Referring to the woman's nose as a "tower of Lebanon" (frankincense) is reminiscent of the reference to the man's cheeks as "beds [towers] of spice" (5:13). Besides the similarity in sound, there is a color connection between these two words: the cliffs of the Anti-Lebanon Mountain range are chalk colored and frankincense is white. This color connection may in fact be the reason for the linguistic correspondence. Finally, the tower mentioned in this comparison faced Damascus, just as the promontories of the mountain range fall steeply down to the major road to that city. One can conclude from all of this that the reference here is to an impressive nose, that is white and straight.

124

The image of a mountain is employed once again. This time the mount is Carmel, one of the most majestic elevations in the north of Israel. Though it cannot rival the heights of the Lebanon range, Carmel rises abruptly out of the Plain of Jezreel, giving it an imposing appearance. The heights of Carmel were known for heavily wooded areas and dense vegetation. This metaphor suggests that, as the heights of Carmel dominate the surrounding land, so the woman's head is situated proudly above the rest of her body, her thick tresses a crowning touch to her beauty. Many commentators note the auditory similarity between Carmel and the word for scarlet. Such a play on words links this phrase with the one that follows, a phrase which also describes the woman's hair.

In earlier poems the woman's hair was compared to a flock of black goats streaming down the slopes of Gilead (4:1; 6:5). Though this metaphor is quite different, the referent of the comparison is the same. The woman's hair is deep-colored and flowing. Here it is likened to threads that hang from a weaver's loom (cf. Is 38:12), threads of a rich purple color. The purple coloring implied most likely came from the murex shellfish, a sea creature that was found in abundance on the Mediterranean coast and whose shades ranged from red to violet or blue-black. The earlier allusion to scarlet would correspond to this reference to color. The shades suggested here need not imply that the woman's hair was dyed. They may simply refer to its highlights, caught by light, that shimmer and ripple as she moves.

The final phrase of this verse is difficult to interpret. The image that it generates is curious. According to the Hebrew, the king is trapped in conduits or watercourses, a detail that seems out of place here. However, there are some literary links in this phrase with what precedes it, thus throwing light on its meaning. The precious purple coloring mentioned earlier in the verse is generally associated with royalty. Hence the mention of a king. The conduits suggest streams of water.

125

The reference here is probably to the rippling effect of the woman's flowing hair. The king, another allusion to the royal fiction, is held captive by its radiance and its seductive appearance.

Although they are used for poetic force, the geographic references in this *wasf* cannot be overlooked. Heshbon, Lebanon, Damascus and Carmel are all situated on or near one of the important international highways that traversed the land of Israel. Heshbon is located where the King's Highway passes to the north to Phoenicia. A second road, the Via Maris, winds its way around Mount Carmel, passing the Anti-Lebanon and Lebanon ranges on its way to Damascus. Along these travel routes came the caravans carrying the spices, precious metals, and rich dyes referred to in many of the poems of the Song. All of this demonstrates the international character of the poems.

The *wasf* begins by addressing the woman as a royal personage (v. 2) and concludes with a reference to a king (v. 6), creating a kind of *inclusio*. Although the composite image it produces is unique, it shares certain literary characteristics with other *wasfs*. First, it functions as the reply to a question posed by another person (7:1b; cf. 5:9). Second, as with other *wasfs* before it, it concludes with a comment describing the effect that the charms of the loved one being extolled produces in the one beholding them (cf. 4:6; 5:16). It is easy to see that these poems share a literary function in the Song as a whole.

The Song of the Soul: The specific subject and poetic character of this poem harmonize with a spirituality that is nature-sensitive, inclusive of human sexuality, and attentive to issues of gender mutuality.

First, the dance reveals the woman's own lack of sexual inhibitions. Although there is neither an explicit identification of the nature of the dance nor mention of the motivation that

126

impelled her to perform it, the dance itself was clearly provocative. Either the character of its movement or the costume worn during its rendition or both of the above revealed parts of her body that were normally concealed from view. Nothing in the poem suggests that she was either embarrassed by her sexuality or intent on flaunting it. The dance appears to be as genuine and unaffected as are the features of the natural world that are employed to describe it.

The woman performs the dance, but its description is from the man's point of view. The details that he reports reveal the amorous nature of his interest. His appreciation of the dance is more than artistic, it is sensual. However, there is nothing in his preoccupation that can be considered lewd. He does not fantasize about how the woman's body can satisfy his sexual desires. Instead, he compares its appeal with the unfeigned enchantment of nature. Like the woman, the man is neither inhibited by her or his sexuality nor obsessed by it. It is a reality of human maturity, and though it influences the character of the relationship between women and men, it is not portrayed as an overpowering drive that neither can control.

Dance is a marvelous metaphor for life. Both spring from the balance between spontaneity and control; both require sensitivity to ebb and flow. There is a variety of dance steps just as there are various aspects to life. Sometimes we move slowly, at other times our stride and gestures are rapid and staccato. Both life and dance have great diversity, making the experience exciting and frightening.

Dance is also a metaphor for the rhythmic movement of the universe, the forcefulness of its expansion and the reliability of its symmetry. The universe follows a melody unknown to us and it creates a spectacle that mesmerizes us with its predictability on the one hand and its novelty on the other. Its synergism reveals the interdependence of its various parts and the attentiveness with which each part faithfully follows the music. In a very real sense, rhythm is in our blood.

The metaphors used in the *wasf* turn to the richness and appeal of nature for illustrations of the exceptional comeliness of the woman's physical makeup. The gentle tawny color of wheat, the pristine white of ivory, the glistening accents of sunlight and the dense mountain growth characterize the delicate coloring of her body and the shimmering brilliance and thickness of her hair. The mysterious quality of deep tranquil water aptly describes her eyes, and the sharp decline of rock her stately nose. All of these images reveal a keenly observant eye and a profound appreciation for the splendor that the natural world exhibits. In his desire to extol the enchanting charms of the woman he loves, the man appeals to this splendor.

Finally, the portrait sketched in this poem is of a woman who is self-possessed. When called upon to dance, she does not obey blindly but instead asks for reasons for such a performance. There is nothing in the poem to suggest that, though provocative, her dance is inappropriate or unconventional. She is called on to dance, and when she does, she is in complete control. She appears to be unafraid of her own sensuality or of the sexual interest that it can generate. At the same time, she does not seem to be manipulating others with it. It is a fact of human maturity and she does not exploit it.

The Delights of Love (7:7-10)

G   ⁷How beautiful you are, how pleasing,
          my love, my delight!
      ⁸Your very figure is like a palm tree,
          your breasts are like clusters.
      ⁹I said: I will climb the palm tree,
          I will take hold of its branches.
      Now let your breasts be like clusters of the vine
          and the fragrance of your breath like apples,
      ¹⁰And your mouth like an excellent wine—

B   that flows smoothly for my lover,
          spreading over the lips and the teeth.

The song of admiration (7:7-10) that follows the *wasf* begins with an exclamation of praise of the woman. She is beautiful and pleasing like no other (v. 7a). The rest of the verse has been translated in various ways. Most interpreters believe that the double adjectival exclamation (beautiful and pleasing) is followed by a double address (love and delight). Although the Hebrew for love is an abstract form of the word, they maintain that it refers to the woman rather than to love itself. The second term of address they translate variously as "daughter of delights," "delightful daughter" or simply "delight." Because the ensuing poem describes the physical delights that the woman's body provides and that the man hopes to enjoy, other interpreters maintain that, instead of being terms of endearment addressed to the woman, the words "love" and "delight" refer to the pleasures of lovemaking. The celebration of the woman's beauty found in the preceding *wasf* here moves into anticipation of enjoying the delights that her alluring body can afford.

This rhapsody of love continues with a litany of similes that compare the woman's charms to the fruits of the earth. Her stature is like a palm tree; her breasts like its clusters. The date palm, so important in the Near East as a source of nourishment, was frequently used to symbolize the tree of life. Earlier the woman compared her loved one to an apple tree that provided both shade and the taste of sweetness (2:3), as well as to a cedar of Lebanon, a tree renowned for its firmness and enduring character (5:15). Here the image of a fruitful tree provides the man with features that represent her desirability. The fruit of the date palm was produced high above its tall stately trunk, making it relatively inaccessible, another image of the reclusive disposition of the woman. The image suggests that both the fruit of the tree and the breasts of the woman are mature and enticing.

The palm metaphor continues as the man muses about climbing the tree and enjoying the delectability of the fruit of the dates that cluster at its top. Climbing the tree in order to procure the dates was the way harvesting was done. In fact, the verse (v. 8) alludes to three different harvest periods: dates in August, grapes from August to September, apples during autumn. Although the love shared by the woman and the man is described as fresh and youthful as springtime (cf. 2:11-13), the maturity of the couple, at least of the woman, is alluded to through the use of harvest imagery. It should be noted that, while this imagery is clearly erotic, it does not suggest explicit genital activity. The woman's sexually developed body does not seem to be desired by the man for the sake of reproduction, but for the sensual satisfaction that both he and she herself can derive from it.

What follows in the poem is a free association of images. The cluster of dates suggests a cluster of grapes. Both dates and grapes are desired for their sweet taste. Sweet taste is coupled with the sweet smell, first of apples (passionate fruit) and then of the woman's nose (breath). Reference to her nose may suggest either nose-kissing or passionate breathing, both of which can be appropriately linked to the sweetness of the palate of her mouth (cf. 5:16; also 2:3; 4:11). The allusion is to deep, passionate, open-mouth kissing. The link between wine and erotic pleasure is made frequently throughout the Song (cf. 1:2, 4; 4:10; 5:1; 7:3). All of these images are descriptive of her sensuous mouth, clearly one of the most erogenous areas of the human body.

The Song of the Soul: As with the preceding *wasf*, this poem lends itself to a contemporary spirituality interpretation. First, its erotic character is apparent. The man is intent on achieving satisfaction that is sexual but not explicitly genital. The woman's mature and enticing breasts are compared first to the luscious fruits of the date palm and then to the succulent grapes of the vine. The description of her kisses suggests that they are deep, passionate and quite erotic. Although the poem relates the pleasure that the man hopes to enjoy, the amorous behavior that he recounts is of the kind that both the woman and the man would savor. Fondling and tasting her breasts and passionate kissing are mutually enjoyable. The passion described here is of the kind that gives pleasure to both lovers.

The nature-sensitive character of the poem is evident in the choice of metaphors with which it abounds, metaphors that appeal to several of the senses. The woman's stature is imposing; her breasts are full and enticing to both touch and taste. Her breath is sweet-smelling; her kisses intoxicating like wine. The metaphorical character of this particular poetic description provides a glimpse into the abundant reserve of sensations that the natural world can provide human imagination. It is only because this world, in all of its glorious manifestations, exercises such a power of attraction over human beings, that various aspects of it make suitable comparisons to human features. The woman is as tantalizing as the world is.

Furthermore, just as the awesome beauty, exhilarating sensations and mature fruitfulness of the world are naturally attractive, so are the physical features of the woman. There is nothing untoward in the man's fascination with her or in his desire to enjoy the pleasures of her charms. The attraction is instinctive and unfeigned. There is nothing inappropriate or exploitative here. Female beauty and the sexual attraction that it engenders are an authentic dimension of the world of nature.

There is a natural attraction here not unlike the power of gravity. In the world of nature, things are drawn to each other. They seem to be so moved by a force placed within them at the time of their creation. So it is with us. We are drawn to each other by an attraction that may lie dormant for a time, but which comes alive when ignited by the flame of love. Physical, intellectual and spiritual attraction are God-given forces, not to be denied, not to be abused.

Mutual Possession and Enjoyment (7:11-14)

[11]I belong to my lover
  and for me he yearns.
[12]Come, my lover, let us go forth to the fields
  and spend the night among the villages.
[13]Let us go early to the vineyards, and see
  if the vines are in bloom,
If the buds have opened,
  if the pomegranates have blossomed;
There will I give you my love.
[14]The mandrakes give forth fragrance,
  and at our doors are all choice fruits;
Both fresh and mellowed fruits, my lover,
  I have kept in store for you.

The next poem (7:11-14), found on the lips of the woman, continues the use of nature imagery in its proposal of mutual passionate enjoyment. The poem itself begins and ends with an address to the man identified as beloved (*dôd*, vv. 11, 14). The opening address is a variation of a familiar refrain: "My lover belongs to me and I to him" (2:16 and 6:3). This text reads literally: "I am my beloved's and his desire is toward me." The modification made here fits the poetic context, where the focus has been on the man's desire for the woman (vv. 7-10). The explicit articulation of that desire now becomes part of the refrain.

The word for desire is found in only two other places in the Bible, both in the Book of Genesis. In all three cases the syntactic structure is the same; the prepositional phrase identifying the object of desire occurs before the word in question, thus indicating emphasis. In the first instance (Gn 3:16), the woman's desire is for her husband; in the second (Gn 4:7), sin's desire is for Cain. Because of the strength of the desire, the man is either expected to or seizes the opportunity to rule over the desire (4:7 and 3:16 respectively).

132

Here the man's desire is for the woman. In light of the similarity in wording, it should be understood as the others were. One would expect here as well that there would be some statement about ruling over the desire. This is where the similarity ends. Rather than suggest that this particular desire should in some way be controlled, the poem indicates that there is a balance here. Not only does the woman not seek to take undue advantage of the man's desire for her, but in fact she acknowledges that he in turn has some control over her. The lovers mutually possess each other. Furthermore, this possessing is done, not in a domineering fashion, but in the manner of self-giving love. The domination of the man over the woman, so clearly stated in the Genesis passage, is overturned here, and it is done with a refrain that falls between one poem that features a tree (vv. 7-10) and another that features a garden (vv. 11-14).

The woman continues with an invitation to the man to go out with her to a place where they can enjoy their love (vv. 12-13). Her introductory imperative, "Come, my lover" (*dôdi*), is followed by four verbs in rapid succession, all in plural cohortative form: "let us go forth," "let us spend the night," "let us go out," "let us see." The first three verbs, which appear to be parallel statements, invite movement toward a place; the fourth is an invitation to observe the signs of spring.

There is some disagreement as to the meaning of the second phrase, "let us spend the night." The word that follows can be translated as villages or as henna bushes. There are several reasons why henna bushes seems to be the better translation. First, the similarity between these verses (7:12f) and earlier verses (1:13f) is unmistakable. Secondly, there (1:14) and elsewhere (4:13), the Hebrew word is translated as henna. Finally, the phrases that precede and follow this particular one (7:12b,13a) suggest parallel meaning in all three phrases.

The man is invited to go out into the fields. The word used

denotes an open uncultivated area outside of a walled city. This was where the vineyards were normally planted, and where henna, with its blossoms that clustered like grapes, was frequently found. He is further invited to lie in the henna. While the verb normally means "to spend the night," the sexual implications of this proposal are obvious. Finally, an invitation into the vineyards brings to mind all of the earlier sensuous references and allusions to vineyards (1:14; 2:15; 8:12), vines (2:13; 6:11; 7:8), and wine (1:2, 4; 4:10; 5:1; 7:9; 8:2).

The purpose of the visit to the vineyards is to observe the progress of spring growth. In addition to the linguistic links already made between this passage and the one describing the woman's visit to the nut orchard (6:11), the invitation has much in common with the man's earlier request that the woman come out into the burgeoning new life of springtime (2:10-13). There are differences as well. In the earlier passage (2:10-13), spring had indeed already awakened, and the man hoped that its surge of life would also awaken the love of the couple. In this verse (7:13), the love of the woman and man has already been well established, and the awakening of springtime reflects love's surge of life.

There, in that place of flowering life, the woman will give the man her love. The word for love is plural in form and appears in other places, where its sweetness is said to surpass that of wine (1:2, 4; 4:10). This suggests the physical enjoyment of love or lovemaking, and not merely a sentiment of love, profound as it may be. There is a play on words between "my love" (*dôdi*) and mandrakes (*dûday*), the beautiful purple flowers that produce juicy, golden fruit. This exotic plant was considered an aphrodisiac and thought to be an aid in effecting pregnancy (cf. Gn 30:14-16). The fragrance that it gives off is quite distinctive and, presumably, provocative. Once again, there is an allusion to the erotic nature of the sense of smell (cf. 1:2f, 12-14; 4:10, 14, 16; 5:5).

Commentators have been puzzled by the remark in this

poem about the doorways (v.14), since all of the references here have been to open spaces. Is this an allusion to the house of the woman's mother that is mentioned in what follows (cf. 8:2), to the natural arbor suggested at the very beginning of the Song (1:17)? It is not clear. What is clear is that these doorways are hung with all of the choicest fruits. Since in an earlier poem the choicest fruits were really the physical charms of the woman (cf. 4:13, 16), the same meaning can be presumed here. The abundance of the fruits is seen in the phrase that follows. "New and old" is a literary construction called merism, a form that implies totality by naming opposing poles (e.g., good and evil, north and south, left and right, etc.). The poles set the parameters of the object under consideration; the merism includes whatever is between these poles. The woman has already promised to make love (7:13). Here she declares that she has laid up the pleasures of lovemaking for her beloved (*dôd*).

The Song of the Soul: This poem fosters several themes identified with values that influences a contemporary spirituality. First, the sexual connotations are plain and unabashed. This is an invitation to a romantic tryst. Although the suggested settings for lovemaking are somewhat removed from places of habitation, they are out in the open spaces of nature. Most likely, such withdrawal from residential areas is more for the sake of privacy than secrecy. There is a sense of freedom and spontaneity here, not furtiveness and deception. As has been seen throughout all of the other poems, sexual vitality is as natural as any other life force found in nature. Pursuing it and enjoying it are as normal as is relishing any of the other delights of the world.

The mutuality of the devotion of the lovers is explicitly stated in the opening refrain: "I am his and he is mine." Here there is no trace of gender domination; there is no sexual exploitation; there is no minimizing of the other. There is

135

only reciprocal desire and shared anticipation. Although the initiative is the woman's, it is clear that the man is an equal partner in this love and a willing participant in the tryst.

There is probably no more comforting phrase that lovers can proclaim than, "I am his and he is mine." It bespeaks both belonging and guardianship. It means that you are not alone; you have found a partner. You have been freed from isolation without relinquishing your autonomy, and you have assumed responsibility for another without claiming ownership. It gives you an identity, and it asserts that you are a major part of the identity of another. We recognize, as did God, that it is not good for us to be alone. This phrase states that we have found a suitable partner, one who is bone of our bone and flesh of our flesh; and it is very good.

Finally, the poem is replete with nature-sensitive imagery. The fields, the henna and the vineyards are not only the venues that invite lovemaking; in a sense their vibrancy encourages and mirrors it. The budding and blossoming are suggestive of life that cannot contain itself but must constantly strain forward. The tastes and smells are themselves intoxicating and provocative, arousing the senses and inviting gratification. Nature is not only a partner in this passionate relationship; it is the reason for it, the way it is manifested, and the goal toward which it strains.

Free to be Intimate (8:1-4)

> [1] Oh, that you were my brother,
>   nursed at my mother's breasts!
> If I met you out of doors, I would kiss you
>   and none would taunt me.
> [2] I would lead you, bring you in
>   to the home of my mother.
> There you would teach me to give you
>   spiced wine to drink, and pomegranate juice.

³His left hand is under my head
　　and his right arm embraces me.
⁴I adjure you, daughters of Jerusalem,
　　by the gazelles and hinds of the field,
Do not arouse, do not stir up love,
　　before its own time.

This unit concludes with a second song of yearning by the woman (8:1-4). In several ways it possesses strong similarities with two earlier poems (3:1-5; 5:2-8). All three suggest a romantic rendezvous in a house; all three mention precarious encounters with the public; all three end with an adjuration to the daughters of Jerusalem.

The verb "meet" or "find" (v. 1), appears four times in 3:1-4 and three times in 5:6-8, the accounts of the woman's night venture into the city. The optative form with which this poem begins ("O that . . . ," "If only . . .") and the imperfect form of the next verbs ("I would meet you . . . I would kiss you . . . I would lead you . . . I would bring you in . . .") suggest that everything depends upon the fulfillment of the initial wish.

This particular poem moves us out of the rustic setting of the previous poems. The outside referred to here is probably not the out-of-doors of nature, which offers so many potential trysting places, but rather the out-in-public of human community. Mention of the house of the woman's mother signals a place of habitation. These characteristics along with the similarities with the two poems mentioned above suggest that the setting here is a residential area.

The woman longs for the opportunity openly to demonstrate her affection for her lover. To this end, she wishes that he were like a brother to her, one who was born of the same mother and who suckled at the same breasts. It appears that such a familial relationship would allow her to kiss him publicly without being considered a loose woman and then held in contempt (cf. Prv 7:10-13). The amorous desire that

137

this verse relates is understandable. Seized by passion, the woman longs for the freedom to express this passion at will, unfettered by societal restraints.

However, the verse also reveals a concern that is somewhat curious. Earlier poems depicted the woman spurning social conventions, venturing out into the city, alone, and at night (cf. 3:1-4; 5:2-7). In those instances, she demonstrated no anxiety over possible discovery and subsequent social reproach. In one episode, she even endured physical abuse for her unconventional behavior (5:7), but this did not deter her search for her lover. Her only concern then was in finding him. While there is an intimate connection between public acceptance of the love of this couple and the woman's liberty to demonstrate her sentiments at will, here her real interest is in the latter. Public acceptance is secondary, only a means to an end.

The literary construction of the next line (v. 2) has caused certain translators and interpreters to emend the verse in some way. The appearance of two relatively synonymous verbs with no connecting conjunction, a literary construction known as asyndeton, and the apparent incompleteness of the phrase have sometimes resulted in significant reconstruction. The similarity between this verse and 3:4 have led some to prefer the Septuagint reading. It adds a phrase that results in parallel form that corresponds to the earlier verse. However, since asyndetic constructions are found elsewhere in the Song (cf. 2:11; 5:6) such emendation does not seem to be necessary.

Instead, the double verb construction highlights the importance of the mother's house. It is there that the woman will bring her lover; it is there that she will be taught, presumably about love. Because of the similarities in form, the subject of the verb translated "teach" can be either "she," implying the mother, or "you" referring to the man. The first reading would create a correspondence with the literary pattern found in the parallel passage (5:4), namely, a clause that identifies a function that the mother performs. This is an acceptable reading, since it would probably fall to the mother to teach her daughter the appropriate sexual behavior. The second reading fits the literary context of the present poem, wherein the woman is speaking directly to the man. It would certainly not be out of place to suppose that the man might initiate the woman into the arts of lovemaking. Despite this possibility, the first reading (it is the mother who teaches) is preferred here.

Allusions to lovemaking continue through the end of the verse. The woman speaks of offering the man a drink of spiced wine as well as the juice of the pomegranate, two drinks believed to be sensually arousing. The pomegranate and the grape appeared in the previous poem (7:13) as ripening signs of the awakening of springtime. Finally, in Hebrew there is a play on the words "kiss you" (8:1) and "give you to drink" (8:2), which once again equates passionate kisses with intoxicating beverage.

The refrain (vv. 3f) that ends this poem of yearning (8:1-4) and concludes the entire unit (6:4–8:4) repeats phrases already found in 2:6f and 3:4b-6a, and does so in the same order as found in those earlier poems. This repetition, called associative sequence, is the recurrence of groups of words, sentences, or themes in the same order, even though such order does not seem to be required by the literary context or for the development of thought. The first refrain in this sequence (v. 3; cf. 2:6) suggests an amorous embrace. Although the image does conform well to the picture of the passionate lovemaking suggested, its shift from first person singular direct address to third person constitutes a literary break.

The adjuration (v. 4) differs slightly from its earlier appearances (2:7; 3:5). First, the negative adverb, which is usually used in oaths, is replaced by an interrogative pronoun that here functions as a negative. Secondly, reference to the gazelles and hinds is actually omitted in the Hebrew, although added in many English versions as our reference shows. Its omission changes the nature of the phrase, for when there are no objects by which an adjuration is made, it takes on the character of a prohibition. As it stands, it belongs less to the poem, which recounts a passion that does not have to be aroused, than to the entire unit. In that capacity, it functions as its conclusion.

The Song of the Soul: Lovers are often torn between the desire to express their devotion openly and the need that they feel to protect it from judgmental eyes. The intimacy that they share prompts them to search for privacy, even to be secretive. They sometimes devise ways of behaving in public that have very personal meaning known only to each other. They realize that if detected they could be accused of duplicity, but safeguarding the delicacy of love is worth the risk.

The tone of this brief poem resonates with values that influence a contemporary spirituality. While there is very little nature-sensitive imagery in these few verses, the assertiveness of the woman is undeniable and the complementary quality of the human passion depicted is evident. The appreciation for the extravagance of nature is seen in the poem's references to spiced wine and pomegranate juice. Both of these drinks are prized for their ability to excite as well as for their fruity essence. This shows once again the attraction that the world of nature exercises over human beings. Not only is it the source of human nourishment without which life is impossible, but it is the fountain of so much that brings human enjoyment as well.

The woman is the determining agent in this poem. It is her longing that is recounted, her familial situation that is represented, her behavior that sets the stage for mutual pleasure. She is the one who would initiate the kiss that they would both enjoy. Though it is the man who would embrace her, she is the one who would be caressed, a fondling that

140

would be mutually gratifying. The woman's passion directs both her and the man she loves. It is a passion that cannot be easily hidden away, but that must be allowed to reveal itself in the open. Those who know of it, the daughters of Jerusalem and those in the house of her mother (?), are expected to respect its spontaneous display.

VII

The Mystery of Love

This final unit is a composite of disparate questions and poems with catchwords that recall earlier scenes from the Song and with declarations that bring the entire collection to a conclusion. It is introduced by a rhetorical inquiry of admiration (8:5a) from an identified speaker that stands without an answer. The poem that follows (vv. 5b-7), spoken by the woman, is an expression of yearning followed by a characterization in praise of love that is considered by many the highpoint of the entire Song. There is a short dialogue between the brothers and the woman (vv. 8-10), a kind of boast from the man (vv. 11-12), and a final exclamation first from the man and then from the woman, expressing their mutual yearning (vv. 13-14).

The Apparition (8:5a)

D   5a Who is this coming up from the desert,
      leaning upon her lover?

There is an abrupt change of setting. The countryside of the previous scene is here replaced by the wilderness. The question that opens this unit (v. 5a) is rhetorical, it does not require an answer. It is framed in a formula that appears in two earlier poems (3:6; 6:10). In each of these three cases the query is clarified by the description that follows. The first

142

part of this question contains the Hebrew expression identical with that found in 3:6. In both of these two instances, it follows an adjuration directed to the daughters of Jerusalem. In the earlier poem, it was the litter of Solomon that came up from the wilderness. Here is it the woman, the one who is the focus of attention throughout this final unit. The second part of the verse contains a word found nowhere else in the Bible, the root of which means "to support." The woman does not come out of the wilderness alone; the couple comes out together.

There are several features in this half-verse that link it to other parts of the Song. First, the question itself is a repetition of the earlier formula (3:6; 6:10). Secondly, although there is a difference between the countryside (7:11) and the wilderness (8:5a), in post-exilic prophetic writings, they are frequently associated with each other (Is 43:20; Ez 29:5; Jl 1:19f; 2:22). Finally, the image of the man supporting the woman is found both here and in the previous poem (8:3). All of this suggests that the poet is deliberately making connections, bringing this collection of poems to a conclusion.

The Character of Love (8:5b-7)

G   ^{5b}Under the apple tree I awakened you;
      it was there that your mother conceived you,
      it was there that your parent conceived.

B   ⁶Set me as a seal on your heart,
      as a seal on your arm;
  For stern as death is love,
      relentless as the nether world is devotion;
      its flames are a blazing fire.
  ⁷Deep waters cannot quench love,
      nor floods sweep it away.
  Were one to offer all he owns to purchase love,
      he would be roundly mocked.

The remainder of the verse sets the stage for the statement regarded by many commentators as the climax of the entire Song. It too contains links with earlier poems. In one of these poems, the apple tree, a symbol of the man, offers shade under which the woman can delight in the sweetness that the man provides (2:3, 5). Here, the woman is the actor, awakening the man. This awakening should be understood in the sense of the arousal of passion, not merely rousing from sleep. Just as the woman frequently returns in thought to her mother's chamber, the place where she was conceived (3:4; 8:2), there to enjoy the erotic pleasures that accompany sexual union, so here she associates the couple's trysting site with the place where the man was conceived. Linking the places where their mothers conceived with the sites of their passionate trysts connects the new love that is theirs with the idea of new life.

The longing of the woman is stated in imperative form: "Set me as a seal." Seals were symbols of personal identity frequently worn around the neck so as to be near the heart (cf. Gn 38:18), on the hand as a ring (cf. Jer 22:24; Hg 2:23), or on arm bands. The woman's desire to be carried near the heart of her lover is understandable. However, since she speaks of a seal on his arm as well as one around his neck, the place of the seal seems less important than the meaning for which it stood. The woman is not speaking of an amulet worn for protection or of some form of jewelry worn as adornment. Instead, she is referring to a kind of personal seal which had deep symbolic significance. It represented the owner's authority, honor, very identity.

The implications of this request are profound. The woman is asking to be identified with the man's very identity, first sealed by it herself and then becoming the public expression of it. She wants the relationship between herself and the man she loves to be as intimate, as inseparable and as distinctive as is the link between the man and the personal seal that marks his identity. Finally, a seal is used as a public mark of identification. Although the woman has acknowledged that public display of affection can result in social disdain (cf. 8:1), she has not really allowed such disapproval to impede her pursuit of her lover (cf. 3:2f; 5:6f). Here as well, she seems unafraid of public disclosure. All she wants is union with the one she loves.

The metaphors that follow (vv. 6b-7) all describe some dimension of deep and lasting love. The text speaks not of the woman's or the man's or the couple's particular love, but of love in general. Though each relationship of love is unique, the experience of the consuming character of the love that she shares with the man gives the woman insight into the nature of love itself. In poetic parallel construction she testifies that love is strong, irresistible as is death; exclusive devotion is resolute, relentless as is sheol. She is not claiming that love will eventually conquer death, or even that love and death are vying with each other in some kind of contest. Rather, she is saying that just as death and sheol, the netherworld, are tenacious and undaunted in the pursuit of their goals, so love and exclusive devotion are single-minded and undeterred in the pursuit of theirs.

The intensity of love is the focus of the next comparison. It states that this fierce love gives off flames or sparks or darts of fire that flare with an elemental force. The meaning of the final word in this description of the flashes of fire has long been debated. Since the word ends with a shortened form of the name of Israel's God (YHWH), it has sometimes been rendered "flame of God." The form frequently functions as an emphatic particle denoting intensification, thus yielding the translation "raging flame." The ending also serves as the adjectival form of a superlative, "fiercest flame." However the word is translated, the form indicates that the flame generated by the love being described is like no other flame.

The imagery turns from the element of fire to its opposite, water. The phrase "many waters" is an idiom that denotes the sea or violent disturbances in it. It carries the sense of chaotic cosmic waters. This mythological connotation is also present in the parallel phrase that speaks of rivers of floods. The metaphor declares that neither the chaotic sea nor the raging floods can overwhelm deep and consuming love. Such love is steadfast and resistant to death, flame, and water (for the use of this language describing eschatological security see Is 43:2).

There is another mythological dimension to each of these elementary forces of nature. Mot (death), Resheph (flame), Yam (sea), Nahar (river, flood) are all names of ancient Canaanite gods of chaos and destruction. Some ancient creation myths tell of, and extant artifacts depict, cosmic battles among the gods. In them, weather-gods using arrows of lightning wage war against death, the sea and the river, and these gods emerge triumphant. The use of this imagery in the characterization of love is quite significant. It implies that human love, like the mythological weather-gods, is able to withstand even the forces of chaos.

The section ends with a statement insisting that it is futile to try to buy love, even if one is willing to risk all else to acquire it. Although many commentators believe that this phrase is a misplaced fragment of another poem containing no mythological allusions and inappropriately appended to this particular piece of poetry, it does enjoy a certain amount of correspondence to what precedes it. The earlier metaphors all characterized human love as beyond the power and control of cosmic forces of chaos. If this is the case, then surely no material wealth, regardless of its nature or its measure, can be considered a medium of exchange for the acquisition of love. In other words, if love cannot be overwhelmed by powers beyond the human domain, it certainly cannot be bought with mere human resources. To think otherwise is to be foolish and deserving of scorn.

The Little Sister (8:8-10)

[8] "Our sister is little
    and she has no breasts as yet.
What shall we do for our sister
    when her courtship begins?
[9] If she is a wall,
    we will build upon it a silver parapet;
If she is a door,
    we will reinforce it with a cedar plank."
[10] I am a wall,
    and my breasts are like towers.
So now in his eyes I have become
    one to be welcomed.

Believing that the Song really ended with the preceding poem in praise of love, many commentators consider the rest of the chapter to consist simply in miscellaneous appendices. Because of ambiguities within the text itself, this section (vv.8-10) has been variously interpreted. For example, in every other instance where the woman is referred to as sister, it is the man who is using that designation as a term of endearment (cf. 4:9, 10, 12; 5:1, 2). The plural form of the possessive pronoun used here and the concern that is expressed in the poem make it clear that the man is not the speaker.

Most likely the speakers are the brothers who were mentioned in one of the earliest sections of the Song (cf. 1:6). Their concern for their sister arises out of their sense of responsibility for her marriageability, a responsibility that is a well-established custom (cf. Gn 24:29-60; 34:6-17). The woman is called "little" sister, one with small breasts. Her retort (v. 10) suggests that their concern is less with her age or the size of her breasts than with what these characteristics imply, namely, her sexual immaturity and unreadiness for marriage (cf. Ez 16:7).

The two conditional phrases that follow (v. 9) are in strict parallel construction, each word of the first clause having a counterpart in the second. Some commentators believe that the parallelism is synonymous, containing analogous metaphors. They consider wall and door as restrictions that prohibit entrance. Other interpreters read it as antithetic parallelism with metaphors of opposite meaning. They agree that the wall prevents access, but they believe that the door allows it. Since the Hebrew word is door and not doorway (cf. 7:14b), the first interpretation is preferred here. Whichever interpretation is adopted, the intent of the metaphors is fundamentally the same. The brothers feel responsible for the sexual conduct of their sister and they will take measures that they think are appropriate to safeguard her marriageability.

Comparing her to a wall or an enclosure, the brothers announce that they would not only fortify her with a turret, thus securing her integrity, but they would use silver in its construction, thus enhancing that integrity. Comparing her to a door, they plan to reinforce the door with boards of cedar, wood that is both strong and precious. Both metaphors reflect the woman's inaccessibility and her brothers' willingness to reinforce that inaccessibility, while at the same time making her even more desirable.

The woman protests her brothers' exaggerated protectiveness (v. 10). She is indeed an inaccessible wall, but she has command of that wall and is in need of no gratuitous assistance. Contrary to her brothers' evaluation, she is not sexually immature. In fact, continuing the use of military architectural imagery, she likens her fully developed breasts to towers. She ends her rebuttal stating that it is because of her maturity and the integrity that has been strengthened through it, that the man she loves looks upon her as the one who brings peace. This is the only time that the word peace appears in the Song. It suggests that any tension alluded to throughout the poems has been resolved. It is also a link with the references to Solomon that follow.

The Vineyard of Value (8:11-12)

B   ¹¹Solomon had a vineyard at Baal-hamon;
     he gave over the vineyard to caretakers.
For its fruit one would have to pay
     a thousand silver pieces.
¹²My vineyard is at my own disposal;
     the thousand pieces are for you, O Solomon,
     and two hundred for the caretakers of its fruit.

This short poem (vv. 11-12) is a boasting song. In the Hebrew it is not clear if the speaker is the man or the woman. I believe it is the man It begins with a description of a vineyard owned by Solomon, and then compares the royal vineyard with one that belongs to the man. Although the change in speaker and content clearly set this section off from what immediately precedes it, the poem does not stand isolated from the rest of the Song. In fact, picking up several themes found in earlier poems, it too seems to bring this disparate collection to some kind of closure.

The opening statement, "Solomon had a vineyard," is reminiscent of other narrative poems (cf. Is 5:1; 1 Kgs 21:1). The place of this particular vineyard is difficult to locate. It may in fact be a fictitious site, intended by its name (Baal-hamon means Lord of the Multitude) to highlight its expansiveness and, thus, the wealth of the king. The size of the vineyard required that the king entrusted its keeping to others. The amount of payment received for the fruits of the vineyard (a thousand pieces of silver; cf. Is 7:23) and the share enjoyed by the workers (two hundred) reveals the scope of its yield. The scene sketched is one of tenant farming and sharecropping. This exaggeration may be an instance of the ancient characterization of any royal personage. However, it is a necessary exaggeration that serves here as a comparison, not a description.

In contrast to the king, who shares with others not only

his vineyard but also the fruits that it produces, the man boasts that his own vineyard is for him alone. It may not compare in size or yield with that of the king, but it is his and his alone. Just as the historical king with his many and vast vineyards became the symbol of wealth, so here the vineyard is a literary fiction, a symbol for something else. Earlier the woman was described as a garden, first possessed by herself and then belonging to the man to whom she gave herself (4:12–5:1). Vineyard is a metaphor that carries some of the same meaning. The earlier implied allusions to the woman as a vineyard (1:6; 7:8) are here made obvious.

The themes of the enclosed garden (4:12), the walled city (8:8-10) and this notion of a vineyard at the disposal of the man alone denote the inaccessibility of the woman to all others. This is precisely the man's boast. Solomon may have vaster holdings, but they are not for his exclusive enjoyment. Wealth does not guarantee greater pleasure. In fact, the administration of wealth may even prevent one from enjoying its fruits. The comparison drawn here recalls the final statement of the earlier poem that celebrated love. No amount of wealth can buy love (8:7).

The Final Exchange (8:13-14)

G   13O garden-dweller,
        my friends are listening for your voice,
        let me hear it!

B   14Be swift, my lover,
        like a gazelle or a young stag
        on the mountains of spices!

This section, and the entire Song of Songs itself, concludes on a strange note. This is not because the sense of these last verses (vv. 13-14) is obscure, but because they end rather abruptly, without a sense of closure. Despite this abruptness, the verses do tie together several phrases and themes found in earlier poems. Just as there is reference to certain keepers at both the beginning of the collection (1:6) and at its end (8:11-12), so there is mention of companions in both places (1:7; 8:13). The Hebrew expression that refers to the woman's dwelling place in the garden (8:13) is the same as that which characterizes her as a dove in the cleft of the rocks (2:14). Her exhortation to the man to be swift (8:14) is almost the same wording as that found in an earlier entreaty of hers (2:17). Several of these similarities will be called upon to throw light on the meaning of this ending.

The verses themselves comprise a brief exchange of dialogue between the lovers. The man speaks first, and the woman responds. Earlier poems depicted a walled city (8:8f) or an enclosed vineyard (v. 12). These verses speak of a garden which, presumably, is also enclosed. Why the companions should be listening for the voice of the woman is unclear. The primary focus of the phrase is not their listening, but the listening of the man. It is he who longs to hear her voice. The Hebrew implies that it is the sound of her voice and not any particular message that is the object of his desire.

When she does speak, her words (v. 14) are enigmatic: "Be swift!" The verb does not ask that the man run swiftly *to* something or someone, but that he run *away from*. In the earlier poem mentioned above, the woman urges him to run away like a gazelle or a young stag on the mountain of spices, to run away before day breaks and their lovemaking is discovered (2:17). Similar wording, but without the exhortation to flee, is found in a second poem (4:6), which also includes reference to a mountain of spices. Throughout several poems, spice is used as a metaphor for the charms of the woman (e.g. 5:1; 6:2). All of this suggests that this last verse should be understood in a similar fashion. The woman pleads that the man flee with the swiftness of a gazelle or a young stag on the mountain of spices.

151

Thus the Song of Song ends, not with final consummation of the passionate love that is described throughout its many individual poems, but on a note of separation. As incomplete as this may sound, it is also quite true of authentic love. Human love knows no definitive consummation, no absolute fulfillment. Loving relationships are never complete; they are always ongoing, always reaching for more. Regardless of the quality or frequency of lovemaking, there is always a measure of yearning present.

The Song of the Soul: This final unit brings together all of the threads of values that influence a contemporary spirituality discussed throughout this study: sensitivity to nature; attentiveness to the characterization of the woman; mutuality of a love relationship.

Nature-sensitive imagery is utilized in two very different ways. First, although it does not play a major role here, there is a reference to the garden (8:13), a metaphor for the woman used so frequently throughout the poems (4:12–5:1, 6:2). Instead of comparing her to a garden, this poem likens her to a vineyard. The similarity is obvious. Both natural plots produce fruits that give pleasure to those fortunate enough to have access to them. These fruits captivate with their forms and colors and textures, or intoxicate with their fragrances and their savors. To compare a woman to either of these treasure troves of nature is to extol both her natural beauty and to celebrate the exhilarating pleasure that this beauty can provide.

When we think of the spiritual dimension of the material, we normally think of pristine nature: the gradual awakening of the world to an early sunrise or a brilliant splash of color at dusk; the rhythmic mesmerizing sound of waves or the howl of the wind at night; the smell of spring bloom or of summer rain. The images that come easily to mind are the tranquil pastoral scenes, the carefully arranged flower gardens, the vast ocean scapes.

Without denying the spiritual potential of this kind of beauty, there is also an awesomeness in nature when it is untamed. The fire that burns deep in the heart of the earth, pushing upward only to erupt with a force that can destroy whatever is in its path, the waters that overflow and wash away buildings and sometimes life itself manifest a splendor that is awe-inspiring. There is a spiritual dimension to the elementary character of earth, water, air and fire.

The poet's appreciation of nature is also seen in the references to death, fire and water, the elemental forces over which humankind has little if any power. Appealing to the mythological properties of these forces in metaphorical portrayals of human love implies a profound respect for the power that is theirs. The rudimentary might, the undeterred purposefulness, and the consuming nature of each of these forces become apt metaphors of the character of human love only if these features are held in high esteem.

It is because metaphors can be regarded as functioning reflexively that the vehicles that carry meaning and the referents that receive it reciprocally describe each other. In other words, not only do specific features of the garden and the vineyard and the cosmic forces enhance the descriptions of the woman and of human love in general, but by association the esteem in which the man holds the woman and in which human love itself is held augments the significance in human eyes of the natural phenomena.

The outline of the woman sketched in this short unit reveals traits that correspond to contemporary concerns. It is the woman who awakened the man to love and she did this in a manner that is straightforward, contrary to the stereotype of the passive or passive-aggressive woman. Her use of strong cosmic imagery counters the notion that women prefer soft, uncomplicated explanations that are often lacking in substance. She disagrees with her brothers' judgement of her sexual maturity and the supervision over her that this judgement implies, a brave stand to take for a woman in a patriarchal society. This is a portrait of a self-defining and self-determining woman, one that will be cherished by all today.

The mutuality of the love relationship is clearly delineated here. Neither partner is totally or consistently commanding. Sometimes it is the woman who is dominant, sometimes it is the man. The woman may awaken love, but she also wishes to be identified with the man. The man may refer to the woman as his vineyard, but it is clear that she is so because she has given herself to him, not because he has taken possession of her by force. Finally, the last verses comprise a mutual dialogue of the lovers. He pleads: "My friends are listening for your voice, let me hear it!" She exhorts: "Be swift, my lover!" The poem ends as it began, with mutual admiration and longing.

VIII

The Soul of the Song

The Song of Songs is not merely a collection of erotic love poems. It is certainly that, but for believers it is more. It is religious literature; it is sacred scripture; it is the word of God. As part of the wisdom tradition of Israel, it is authentic teaching containing instruction for righteous living in accord with the order set by God at creation. The Song of Songs has much in common with other books within the wisdom tradition. Like them, it addresses a very profound reality, reality that is integral to every human life. For example, Proverbs offers direction for living a successful life, and Job struggles with the mystery of unexplained suffering. As part of this tradition, the Song addresses the magnificence of the love between a woman and a man.

The wisdom books teach indirectly through poetic depiction. They recount how life works; they portray the consequences of specific human behavior. They relate situations and describe sentiments with which people can easily identify. They do not command; they cajole. All of this is done to encourage a way of living that will provide happiness, well being, shalom. This is the tradition to which the Song of Songs belongs. This is the fundamental goal of its instruction. The heart of its teaching is the ebb and flow, the joys and sorrows of heterosexual love. The soul of its teaching is the ability that such love has to transform the lovers into people who are in tune with the mystery of the natural world, with the dignity of the woman as well as the man, and with

155

the distinctive features of their own mutual passion and commitment.

Reflection on the Song of Songs reveals the nature-sensitive character of the poetry. Whether it is the woman in awe of the strength and splendor of her lover, or the man glorifying her physical charms, the descriptions all call on elements from the natural world to characterize the feature being described. In fact, there is no description that does not rely on nature. Whatever they experience or know, or even desire, is somehow rooted in the natural world. In their moments of ecstasy and in their moments of distress, they cry out in words that reflect something of this wondrous world of which we are all a part.

The Song demonstrates that the human heart is in tune with the heart of the natural world, for it is an offspring of that world. It comes from that world; it is made of that world. It sings its song, and it writhes with its pain. It delights in and shares in its contours and hues, its flavors and scents, its textures and tones, all of its sensations. It holds up the virtues of this world as examples to be emulated: the gentleness of the dove; the reliability of the mountain; the prodigality of natural growth; the protection of night; the encouragement of morning.

When the human heart gives itself to another, it is to another offspring of that world that it gives itself. When the lovers look into each others' eyes, it is nature beholding nature. When they give themselves to each other, it is nature loving nature. It is only fitting, therefore, that poetic imagery move beyond the human for the means of its expression, for it shares a commonality with what is beyond the human. This commonality binds all things together, and enables us to step from one natural realm to another and feel somewhat at home.

The Song's sensitivity to nature teaches all of this. And as it teaches, it calls for an attitude of soul that is transformed by such teaching and a way of being and living that demonstrates it. The soul of the Song stands in awe before the wonders of creation. Love has given it tender eyes and gentle hands, perceptive senses that receive from the world with innocence and relish its treasures with enthusiasm. There is no manipulation here, no exploitation. Instead, there is a realization of dependency, of mutuality, of responsibility.

The lovers revel in the extravagance of the world of which they are a part, the world that captivates them and nourishes their appetites. The garden and the vineyard, both cultivated by human diligence, offer themselves to the couple as places of rendezvous. They also revel in the extravagance of that part of the world which they are. They gaze at each other with tender eyes; they embrace each other with gentle hands. They accept expressions of love with innocence and they relish them with enthusiasm. Their sexual attraction is nature charmed by nature.

The human artistry mentioned in the Song is yet another manifestation of the book's sensitivity to nature. The poems speak of houses and chambers and couches, of cities and towers and fortifications, of clothing and jewelry and banners. All of these are praised for their splendor and usefulness. All of them are made out of the stuff of the earth and are patterned after natural phenomena. The challenge to the artist is to refashion the raw material into an artifact that retains the original character and beauty of the material while creating a new use for it. Art is a twofold manifestation of the richness of the world. It features some particular aspect of natural creation, and it demonstrates the natural creativity of the artist.

By portraying the splendors of the world as it does, the Song of Songs challenges us with its teaching. It calls us to stand in awe before natural creation in all of its diverse manifestations. It bids us deal with this creation familiarly yet tenderly, to engage with it respectfully, to be accountable to it and responsible for it. The Song demonstrates that the world cares, and that it must be cared for.

A second feature of the Song of Songs is the portrait of the woman that it sketches. Both the portrait and the woman are remarkable. The explicitness of the sensuality that is drawn, the extravagance of the imagery that is chosen, the diversity of the metaphors that are employed all contribute to a characterization that is unique in its representation yet familiar as an object of fantasy. However, the woman portrayed here is not a fantasy of the male character of the poems. She is as real as he is. In fact, she may be considered more real than he, for the image of him that we have is filtered through her imagination, and his speech is really her recollection of his words.

Although the heart of the Song is human passion, the way that the ebb and flow of this love is described reveals some interesting things about the woman. She is assertive, taking the initiative in this relationship. She is undaunted, risking misunderstanding and censure as she pursues her love. She is independent, making decisions for herself. She is responsible, being accountable for her actions. She is protective, shielding her lover and the love they share from the prying eyes of others. These are characteristics that traditionally have not been ascribed to women, and if they have been, they appear here in untraditional ways.

This assertive woman is in charge of her own life. She is very active in managing many of the details of the trysts that the lovers enjoy. She gives directions to the daughters of Jerusalem, and she initiates conversation with the sentinels in the city. It is clear that her assertiveness is virtue and not merely willfulness. While she is self-directed, she is also sensitive to situations and to the people within them. Her assertiveness springs from the sexual desire that she experiences and from what she perceives as an appropriate response for the moment.

The woman is undaunted in her pursuit of her goals. She is not intimidated by men, neither her brothers nor those who keep watch over the city at night. She does not allow restrictive social custom to curb her devotion. Convinced of the appropriateness of her quest, she is willing to risk reproach and even physical harm, and she does so without condemning those who observe the custom. She is attentive to the reality of life, in her case the reality of the love that she shares with her lover, and she follows life's promptings, responding in ways that may appear to be daring but which she judges suitable.

The woman asks permission of no one, neither man nor woman. She is independent and self-possessed. She alone charts the course of her pursuit of the man, and then she chooses which means to employ in order to reach him. When it is the man who is in pursuit, she decides by herself how she will respond to him. However, hers is not an egocentric independence; her romantic goals are not selfishly narcissistic. The love relationship is mutual and the interaction between the couple is reciprocal. It is more appropriate to describe them as interdependent. Still, one must possess a certain degree of independence before being able to enter into an interdependent relationship.

Responding to her love in ways that are unconventional, the woman does not blame anyone for the setbacks that arise in her search nor for the physical and emotional distress that she experiences. She takes full responsibility for her actions, and she accepts their consequences without recrimination. She must have been considered trustworthy to some degree by her brothers, for they placed her in charge of vineyards. That she does not appear to have attended to her own vineyard as they would have liked may be an example of how they differed in respect to her self-determination.

Women have traditionally been considered protective of their children and of those who are in any way vulnerable. Such a characteristic is not uncommon. What is unusual here is that she is protective of her lover. This suggests that she perceives some dimension of vulnerability in him, and a corresponding strength in herself to accommodate that vulnerability. Whatever the nature of this vulnerability, she assumes a protective stance in his regard. Furthermore, she assumes this stance outside of the precincts of the home, the customary domain of women.

These virtuous characteristics add depth and color to the portrait of the woman that is sketched in the Song. It is her devotion to the man and her desire to protect and nurture the love that they share that have called forth these admirable qualities. Unlike the other depictions of women found in Israel's wisdom literature, this woman does not serve the agendas of men. Here uniqueness has led some commentators to wonder about the identity of the poets who shaped the original poems or the editor who brought them together. Might they have been women, who wished to offer an image of woman that was different from the conventional one?

If this was the case, it would mean that there were some among the ancients who rejected the point of view of their society and, instead, shared an anthropological perspective closer to one that is popular today, a supposition that is quite hard to demonstrate. While we cannot answer the question with certainty, we can say that such an understanding of women does challenge the prejudiced stereotype out of which contemporary women and men are emerging. It applauds the dignity of women who, though very different from men, have been similarly graced with integrity and strength of character.

The third and final feature of the Song that reflects its soul is the mutual passion and commitment of the couple. While the Song describes love in many ways, it is probably its depiction as an elemental power, the force of which rivals the strength of death itself, that is the most startling. The comparison suggests that love can withstand anything, and that it moves inevitably toward its goal—union with the object of its affection. It is a universal force, rooted in the very makeup of the human person. It comes as it will, develops at its own pace, and ultimately pervades every corner of the human heart. It is most certainly one of the most vibrant forces in the world, transforming people and creating unseen bonds that hold the world together.

In the Song, love enabled both the woman and the man to transcend their personal aspirations in the interest of the other; to endure what appears to have been unimaginable distress for the sake of the other. Love made them fully themselves by making them more than themselves. It fulfilled them as individuals and created a new and unique reality—a couple. The poems show love as an elemental force not unlike that of nature, pushing itself out of the protective shell of winter into the renewing light of spring. In fact, it is the womb that gives birth to the springtime of the soul with all of its fecundity, its vibrant splash of color and exotic array of fragrance. Love is truly a force of life that is as strong as death.

The ebb and flow, the absence and presence and recurring absence of the lover may describe the movement within the poems, but the lovers' realization of belonging to each other is its defining theme. It is not good for woman or man to be alone, for aloneness is detrimental to human well-being. However, the Song shows that a partner, who is bone of the same bone and flesh of the same flesh, can satisfy the desire to belong that is deep within the human heart. Thus the woman and man cling to one another, and they become one. The woman proclaims again and again, "He is mine, and I am his!"

There is clearly a mutuality in the belonging described in the poems; both lovers claim the other as her or his own. There is also an attending exclusiveness; they belong to each other and to no one else. This is particularly evident in the woman's case. She is characterized as a garden enclosed, a fountain sealed to all except her lover. To belong to another is to have given oneself, and what is given to one cannot simultaneously be given to someone else. It is unthinkable that a relationship with the scope and depth and character that is depicted in the Song would not be exclusive.

The explicitness of the imagery in the poems demonstrates that the belonging referred to is unquestionably emotional, profoundly spiritual, and certainly physical. No one of these three aspects is absent, nor is any one of them dominant. Rather, they are three dimensions of the same all-encompassing elemental power of love, a power that permeates every corner of the human soul. As such a love transforms, it integrates. It calls all of the powers and personality traits of the person into play and focuses them on the beloved. One who knows this kind of love can say: "At last, I'm whole!"

These powers and traits are integrated not only because they have a common focus, but also because they affect each other. In the heat of passion, emotions can cause strong physical reaction, and a physical quality can elicit an emotional response. In one poem, the woman is so overwhelmed by her love that she is faint. In another, the man begs her to turn her glance away from him, for he is tormented by it. There is no recognizable religious language in the Song, and so it is difficult to identify the interaction between the spiritual dimension and the emotional and physical dimensions. However, the poems suggest that the qualities of mind and heart that love calls forth effect a transformation that is both emotional and spiritual.

The relationship between sexuality and spirituality is not specifically dealt with in the Song. However, the book's place in the biblical canon implicitly addresses it. Unlike many other ancient Near Eastern cultures, Israel neither mythologized nor sacralized sexuality. The cult of Israel did not include a reenactment of the *hieros gamos*, the sacred marriage of the gods. The God of Israel was beyond the polarity of sexuality, and so sexuality was outside of the realm of the divine. The Song of Songs demonstrates this quite clearly. Erotic love between a woman and a man, with all of the creative life forces that attend it, is a human reality not a divine one.

The Song's inclusion in the biblical canon and its place

along with other wisdom writings mark its religious importance. As stated earlier, the wisdom tradition has a decidedly anthropological interest. It is concerned with universal human experience and the insights that reflection on that experience can produce. These insights have led the wise to conclude that there is a basic order to the world put there by the Creator at creation, and wisdom provides some direction in discovering that order and living successfully within it. Thus, though anthropologically focused, the wisdom tradition is theologically grounded. For the people of Israel, the order designed by God is presumed, and the wisdom teaching of the various books is directed by and toward this order.

Both creation narratives in Genesis note the sexual polarity that was created by God in the beginning. Genesis also states that it was God who said that is was not good to be alone, and it was God who brought the woman and the man together, to cling to each other and to become one flesh. This is the order that was created in the beginning, and this is the goal toward which the God-given sexual drive in women and men presses. The Song of Songs is a collection of poetry that describes creative elemental force and the fruits that it can bring forth. As such, it is a profound spiritual reality.

And so the Song of Songs, with its elaborate descriptions of the joys and woes of heterosexual passion, teaches us that such love has the power to transform lovers into people who are in tune with the mystery of the natural world, with the unique dignity of the human person, and with the distinctive features of mutual passion and commitment. It is a lesson worth learning well.

Works Consulted

Alter, Robert. *The Art of Biblical Poetry*. New York: Basic Books, 1985.

Bergant, Dianne. *The World is a Prayerful Place*. Reprinted. Michael Glazier, Inc., Collegeville, MN: Liturgical Press, 1992.

Bloch, Ariel & Chan Bloch. *The Song of Songs* New York: Random House, 1995.

Botterweck, G. Johannes & Helmer Ringgren, eds. *Theological Dictionary of the Old Testament* (Vol. III). Grand Rapids: Eerdmans, 1978.

Brenner, Athalya. *The Song of Songs* (Old Testament Guides). Sheffield: JSOT Press, 1989.

Carr, G. Lloyd. *The Song of Songs* (Tyndale Old Testament Commentaries). Downers Grove, IL: Inter-Varsity Press, 1984.

Copher, Charles B. "The Black Presence in the Old Testament" in *Stony the Road We Trod*, Cain Hope Felder, ed. Philadelphia: Fortress, 1991.

Deckers, M. "The Structure of the Song of Songs and the Centrality of *nepeš* (6:12)" in *A Feminist Companion to the Song of Songs*, Athalya Brenner, ed. Sheffield: JSOT Press, 1993.

Elliott, M. Timothea. *The Literary Unity of the Canticle* (European University Series 23). Bern: Peter Lang, 1989.

Exum, J. Cheryl. "A Literary and Structural Analysis of the Song of Songs" in *Zeitschrift für die alttestamentliche Wissenschaft* 85:47-79, 1973.

Falk, Marcia. *The Song of Songs: A New Translation and Interpretation*. San Francisco: HarperCollins, 1990.

Fox, Michael V. *The Song of Songs and the Ancient Egyptian Love Songs*. Madison, WI: University of Wisconsin Press, 1985.

Gadamer, Hans-Georg. *Truth and Method*. New York: Seabury, 1975.

Gordis, Robert. *The Song of Songs and Lamentations* (revised and augmented edition). New York: KTAV, 1974.

Goulder, Michael D. *The Song of Fourteen Songs*. Sheffield: JSOT Press, 1986.

Keel, Othmar. *The Song of Songs: A Continental Commentary* (Trans. Frederick J. Gaiser). Minneapolis: Fortress, 1994.

Landy, Francis. *Paradoxes of Paradise: Identity and Difference in the Song of Songs*. Sheffield: Almond Press, 1983.

Matter, E. Ann. *The Voice of My Beloved: The Song of Songs in Western Medieval Christianity*. Philadelphia: University of Pennsylvania, 1990.

Merchant, Carolyn. *The Death of Nature: Women, Ecology and the Scientific Revolution*. San Francisco: Harper & Row, 1980.

Murphy, Roland E. *The Song of Songs* (Hermeneia). Minneapolis: Fortress, 1990.

Nelson, James B. "Between Two Gardens: Reflections on Spirituality and Sexuality" in *Between Two Gardens: Reflections on Sexuality and Religious Experience*. New York: Pilgrim Press, 3-15, 1983.

_____. "Reuniting Sexuality and Spirituality," in *The Christian Century* 187-90, 1987.

Pardes, Ilana. *Countertraditions in the Bible: A Feminist Approach*. Cambridge, MA: Harvard University Press, 1992.

Pope, Marvin H. *The Song of Songs* (The Anchor Bible). Garden City, NY: Doubleday, 1977.

Pouget, Guillaume & Jean Guitton. *The Canticle of Canticles.* Tr. Joseph L. Lilly. New York: Declan X. McMullen, 1934.

Principe, Walter. "Toward Defining Spirituality," in *Studies in Religion* (12) 83:127-141, 1983.

Rahner, Karl. "Reflections on the Unity of the Love of Neighbour and the Love of God," in *Theological Investigations* (Vol. VI). Baltimore: Helicon Press, 1969.

Reese, James M. *The Book of Wisdom, The Song of Songs* (Old Testament Message). Wilmington, DE: Michael Glazier, Inc, 1983.

Ricoeur, Paul. *Freud and Philosophy: An Essay on Interpretation* (trans. Denis Savage). New Haven: Yale University Press, 1970.

_____. *Interpretation Theory: Discourse and the Surplus of Meaning* (Eighth Printing). Fort Worth: Texas Christian University Press, 1976.

Robert, Andre, Raymond Tournay & Andre Feuillet. *Le Cantique des Cantiques*. Paris: Etudes Bibliques, 1963.

Rowley, Harold H. "The Interpretation of the Song of Songs," in *The Servant of the Lord and Other Essays* (2nd revised edition). Oxford: Blackwell, 195-245, 1965.

Schneiders, Sandra M. "Theology and Spirituality: Strangers, Rivals, or Partners?" in *Horizons* 13:265-67, 1986.

_____. "Spirituality in the Academy" *Theological Studies* (50) 676-97, 1988.

Shea, William H. "The Chiastic Structure of the Song of Songs," in *ZAW* 92:378-95, 1984.

Snaith, John G. *The Song of Songs* (New Century Bible Commentary). Grand Rapids: Eerdmans, 1993.

Soulen, Richard N. "The *wasf* of the Song of Songs and Hermeneutic," in *Journal of Biblical Literature* 86:183-90, 1967.

Stadelmann, Luis. *Love and Politics: A New Commentary on the Song
of Songs*. New York: Paulist, 1992.

Tournay, Raymond Jacques, O.P. *Word of God, Song of Love: A
Commentary on the Song of Songs*. New York: Paulist Press,
1988.

Trible, Phyllis. *God and the Rhetoric of Sexuality* (Overtures to
Biblical Theology). Philadelphia: Fortress Press, 1978.

Wolff, Hans Walter. *Anthropology of the Old Testament*. Philadelphia: Fortress, 1974.

In the Same Series from New City Press

Mark
From Death to Life
Dennis Sweetland
ISBN 1-56548-117-8, paper, 5 3/8 x 8 1/2, 216 pp.

Matthew
God With Us
Ronald D. Witherup
ISBN 1-56548-123-2, paper, 5 3/8 x 8 1/2, 216 pp.

Romans
The Good News According to Paul
Daniel Harrington
ISBN 1-56548-096-1, paper, 5 3/8 x 8 1/2, 152 pp.

First Corinthians
Building Up the Church
Vincent P. Branick
ISBN 1-56548-162-3, paper, 5 3/8 x 8 1/2, 152 pp.

Paul's Prison Letters
Scriptural Commentaries on Paul's Letters to Philemon,
the Philippians, and the Colossians
Daniel Harrington
ISBN 1-56548-088-0, paper, 5 3/8 x 8 1/2, 136 pp.

Revelation
The Book of the Risen Christ
Daniel Harrington
ISBN 1-56548-121-6, paper, 5 3/8 x 8 1/2, 168 pp.

Daniel
A Book for Troubling Times
Alexander A. Di Lella
ISBN 1-56548-087-2, paper, 5 3/8 x 8 1/2, 232 pp.

To Order Phone 1-800-462-5980
www.newcitypress.com